COOKING FOR ONE:
Air Fryer Cookbook For Beginners

Healthy & Time-Saving Recipes with
a comprehensive Air Fryer Cheat Sheet

Sarah Benton

CONTENTS

INTRODUCTION

At times, cooking a large meal doesn't make sense. Whether you live alone, have guests with dietary restrictions, or simply want to try a new dish without making a big batch, these air fryer cooking for one recipes will be your go-to solution for simple and delicious meals.

Introducing the ultimate guide to air fryer cooking for one - a treasure trove of more than 200 scrumptious, one-serving wonders. Whether you're a newbie to the air fryer or a seasoned pro, this book is your ticket to flavor-packed, single-serve goodness that'll have your taste buds doing the happy dance.

Picture this: crispy, juicy, and guilt-free creations whipped up with the power of hot air. It's like having a mini countertop convection oven at your fingertips! Wave goodbye to greasy deep fryers, space-hogging microwaves, and dusty dehydrators. With the air fryer, you're the culinary maestro, whipping up everything from sweets to crunchy chicken to tasty and healthy fries.

These portioned-scaled recipes will help you save kitchen space, time, money, and avoid unnecessary trips to the drive-through. So get ready to personalize your menu, create delicious and healthy meals, and start air frying!

Choosing an Air Fryer

When you're looking for a new air fryer, there are a few things to consider.

- **First, you'll want to think about how much space it takes up.** Air fryers range from being able to cook single portions to being able to cook enough food for an entire family—so if you live alone, you might not need something as significant as what someone who's cooking for their whole family might want.

- The next thing to look at is **how many are you in your household and how much food they eat.** If you're the only person who eats in your home, then a small air fryer that's designed for single-person use will probably suffice. But you'll want something more extensive if you have kids or friends who are always over for dinner or snacks.

- Also, **consider whether or not you'll be using the appliance solely for cooking chicken or other types of food—or whether this will be one of many uses** (like frying crispy sweet potato wedges!). If it's going to be used primarily for chicken and fries, then look at what cooking settings the air fryer has - some only heat up on one setting while others have multiple options like "bake" and "broil."

Welcome to the wonderful world of air fryers!

Air fryers are **the best way to get crispy, delicious food without using a ton of oil**. They're also **effortless to use,** especially if you go for the recipes in this book.

The first step is understanding what makes an air fryer work. Air fryers don't heat up like other ovens do—instead, they combine hot air and infrared heat to create rapid convection cooking. That means that instead of using oil, you can just let your food cook in its juices and absorb natural oils from the outside as it cooks.

Air Frying Tips and Tricks

Air frying is a great way to cook food, but there are some things you might not be aware of. Here are some tips and tricks to help you make the most of your air fryer!

- **The best way to get crispy skin and tender on the inside is to slightly precook the chicken in boiling water for 5-10 minutes before putting it in the air fryer.** This allows the fat to render out of the skin, giving you a super-crispy crust without adding extra fat (like butter) when cooking in the air fryer.

- If you're going for a more traditional fried taste, try adding some flour or cornstarch **coating along with seasonings and spices.** This will give your the food that extra crunchy texture and unique flavor that we all love about fried foods!

- **Always pat dry your the meat or chicken before seasoning it and placing it into your air fryer basket!** That will help ensure that all those delicious seasonings stick to your meat instead of sliding off into the oil as soon as you start cooking!

- **Don't overcrowd your basket with food!** It's better for both cooking times AND for preventing oil splatters that can burn yourself or ruin something.

Top 3 Reasons why air fried food is healthy and delicious

1. *Crispy Texture:* Air frying creates a delectable, crispy exterior on foods, similar to deep-frying, but with significantly less oil. This texture adds a delightful crunch that is irresistible.

2. *Retained Moisture:* The circulating hot air in air fryers helps lock in the natural moisture of ingredients, keeping them tender and juicy. This ensures that your meals remain succulent and flavorful, whether it's a piece of meat or a vegetable.

3. *Even Cooking:* Air fryers use a powerful fan to circulate hot air, ensuring even cooking on all sides of the food. This results in a consistent and perfectly cooked interior, contributing to its overall deliciousness.

What about Fried Veggies, Fries and Finger Foods

Fried finger foods are a delicious way to spice up your next party or get-together.

Instead of the standard chips and dip, try frying up some vegetable slices and serving them with ranch or blue cheese dressing. You can make them in advance, so they're easy to store and serve when needed!

We love frying up sweet potato fries with a bit of cinnamon. They're great for eating with a sandwich or burger!

To Wrap it up

There are countless ways to prepare various meals, and it's never just the monotonous routine. Whether it's chicken, beef, or fish, they can all be combined in diverse meal combinations. That's the inspiration behind this cookbook! Inside, you'll discover some of our cherished recipes that spotlight these ingredients in possibly newfound ways for you. This cookbook has everything you need to get started on your own journey of creating delicious and healthy meals with your air fryer.

Let's have fun!

BREAKFAST & SWEETS

Easy Hard-Boiled Eggs

Serves: 1 | Total Time: 15 minutes

Ingredients

2 medium eggs

Directions

Start by preheating your air fryer to 250°F. Put the eggs in the air fryer basket. Air Fry for 12-15 minutes. Prepare an ice water bath. When the eggs are ready, transfer them to the ice water to cool and cut the cooking for 5-10 minutes. Then, peel the eggs and serve.

Sweet Blueberry French Toast Sticks

Serves: 1 | Total Time: 20 minutes

Ingredients

2 bread slices, cut into strips
1 tablespoon butter, melted
2 small eggs
1 tablespoon milk

1 tablespoon sugar
½ teaspoon vanilla extract
1 cup fresh blueberries
1 tablespoon lemon juice

Directions

Start by preheating your air fryer to 380°F. After laying the bread strips on a plate, sprinkle some melted butter over each piece. Whisk the eggs, milk, vanilla, and sugar, then dip the bread in the mix. Place on a wire rack to let the batter drip. Put the strips in the air fryer and Air Fry for 5-7 minutes.

Use tongs to flip them once and cook until golden. With a fork, smash the blueberries and lemon juice together. Spoon the blueberry sauce over the French sticks. Serve immediately.

Green Vegetable Omelet

Serves: 1 | Total Time: 20 minutes

Ingredients

¼ cup chopped broccoli, lightly steamed
1 tablespoon grated cheddar cheese
2 eggs

¼ cup steamed kale
1 green onion, chopped
Salt and black pepper to taste

Directions

Start by preheating your air fryer to 360°F. In a bowl, beat the eggs. Stir in kale, broccoli, green onion, and cheddar cheese. Transfer the mixture to a greased baking dish and Bake in the fryer for 15 minutes until golden and crisp. Season to taste and serve immediately.

Almond Flour Pumpkin Porridge

Serves: 1 | Total Time: 10 minutes

Ingredients

1 teaspoon pumpkin seeds

1 teaspoon chopped pecans

1 teaspoon quick-cooking oats

1 tablespoon pumpkin purée

2 diced pitted dates

¼ teaspoon chia seeds

¼ teaspoon dried berries

½ teaspoon butter

2 teaspoons pumpkin pie spice

¼ cup honey

1 tablespoon almond flour

¼ teaspoon salt

Directions

Start by preheating your air fryer to 350°F. Combine the pumpkin seeds, pecans, oats, pumpkin purée, dates, chia seeds, dried berries, butter, pumpkin pie spice, honey, almond flour, and salt in a bowl.

Press the mixture into a greased cake pan. Place the cake pan in the frying basket and Bake for 5 minutes, stirring once. Let cool completely for 10 minutes before crumbling.

Corn Dog Cupcakes

Serves: 1 | Total Time: 30 minutes

Ingredients

1 teaspoon cornbread mix

½ teaspoon granulated sugar

Salt to taste

1 tablespoon cream cheese

1 teaspoon butter, melted

1 small egg

1 minced green onion

¼ teaspoon dried parsley

½ beef hot dog, sliced and cut into half-moons

Directions

Start by preheating your air fryer to 350°F. Combine cornbread, sugar, and salt in a bowl. Whisk cream cheese, parsley, butter, and egg in another bowl. Pour wet ingredients into dry ingredients and mix to combine.

Fold in onion and hot dog pieces. Transfer it into 8 greased silicone cupcake liners. Place it in the frying basket and Bake for 8-10 minutes. Serve right away.

Sweet Almond Tortilla Fritters

Serves: 1 | Total Time: 10 minutes

Ingredients

½ teaspoon granulated sugar

¼ teaspoon ground cinnamon

¼ teaspoon vanilla powder

1 flour tortilla, quartered

½ tablespoon butter, melted

½ teaspoon honey

½ teaspoon almond flakes

Directions

Start by preheating your air fryer to 400°F. Combine the sugar, cinnamon, vanilla powder, and salt in a bowl. Set aside. Brush tortilla quarters with melted butter and sprinkle with sugar mixture.

Place tortilla quarters in the frying basket and Air Fry for 4 minutes, turning once. Let cool on a large plate for 5 minutes until hardened. Drizzle with honey and scatter with almond flakes to serve.

Swiss-Style Omelet

Serves: 1 | Total Time: 20 minutes

Ingredients

2 eggs

1 teaspoon grated Swiss cheese

1 breakfast sausage, sliced

2 bacon strips, sliced

Salt and black pepper to taste

Directions

Start by preheating your air fryer to 360°F. In a bowl, beat the eggs and stir in Swiss cheese, sausages, and bacon.

Transfer the mixture to a baking dish and set in the fryer. Bake for 15 minutes or until golden and crisp. Season and serve.

Cinnamon Apple French Toast

Serves: 1 | Total Time: 30 minutes

Ingredients

2 white bread slices

2 eggs

1 teaspoon cinnamon

½ peeled apple, sliced

1 tablespoon brown sugar

¼ cup whipped cream

Directions

Start by preheating your air fryer to 350°F. Coat the apple slices with brown sugar in a small bowl. Whisk the eggs and cinnamon into a separate bowl until fluffy and thoroughly blended.

Coat the bread slices with the egg mixture, then place them on the greased frying basket. Top with apple slices. Air Fry for 20 minutes, flipping once until the bread is brown nicely and the apple is crispy.

Place one French toast slice onto a serving plate, then spoon the whipped cream on top and spread evenly. Scoop the caramelized apple slices onto the whipped cream and cover with the second toast slice. Serve.

Easy Caramelized Peaches

Serves: 1 | Total Time: 25 minutes

Ingredients

2 pitted peaches, halved

1 tablespoon brown sugar

½ cup heavy cream

½ teaspoon vanilla extract

¼ teaspoon ground cinnamon

1 cup fresh blueberries

Directions

Start by preheating your air fryer to 380°F. Lay the peaches in the frying basket with the cut side up, then top them with brown sugar. Bake for 7-11 minutes, allowing the peaches to brown around the edges. In a mixing bowl, whisk heavy cream, vanilla, and cinnamon until stiff peaks form.

Fold the peaches into a plate. Spoon the cream mixture into the peach cups, top with blueberries, and serve.

Fried Apple with Caramel Sauce

Serves: 1 | Total Time: 15 minutes

Ingredients

1 medium apple, cored

¼ teaspoon cinnamon

¼ teaspoon nutmeg

1 tablespoon caramel sauce

Directions

Start by preheating your air fryer to 350°F. Slice the apple to a 1/3-inch thickness for a crunchy chip. Place in a large bowl and sprinkle with cinnamon and nutmeg. Place the slices in the air fryer basket.

Bake for 6 minutes. Shake the basket, then cook for another 4 minutes or until crunchy. Serve drizzled with caramel sauce and enjoy!

Roasted Pumpkin Rounds

Serves: 1 | Total Time: 35 minutes

Ingredients

¼ pound pumpkin rounds

¼ tablespoon honey

¼ tablespoon melted butter

¼ teaspoon cardamom

¼ teaspoon sea salt

Directions

Preheat the air fryer to 370°F. Mix the honey, butter, cardamom, and salt in a bowl. Toss the pumpkin in the mixture until coated, then put it into the frying basket. Bake for 15-20 minutes, shaking once during cooking, until the edges start to brown and the squash is tender.

Effortless Banana Fritters

Serves: 1 | Total Time: 20 minutes

Ingredients

1 egg

1 tablespoon cornstarch

1 tablespoon bread crumbs

1 banana, halved crosswise

¼ cup caramel sauce

Directions

Start by preheating your air fryer to 350°F. Set up three small bowls. In the first bowl, add cornstarch. In the second bowl, beat the egg. In the third bowl, add bread crumbs. Dip the banana in the cornstarch first, then the egg, and then dredge in bread crumbs.

Put the banana in the greased frying basket and spray with oil. Air Fry for 8 minutes, flipping once around minute 5. Remove to a serving plate and drizzle with caramel sauce. Serve warm.

Crisp Oatmeal with Fruits

Serves: 1 | Total Time: 25 minutes

Ingredients

1 peeled nectarine, chopped

½ peeled apple, chopped

½ cup raisins

1 tablespoon honey

2 tablespoons brown sugar

1 tablespoon flour

2 tablespoons oatmeal

2 teaspoons softened butter

Directions

Start by preheating your air fryer to 380°F. Mix together nectarines, apple, raisins, and honey in a baking pan. Set aside. Mix brown sugar, flour, oatmeal, and butter in a medium bowl until crumbly. Top the fruit in a greased pan with the crumble. Bake until bubbly and the topping is golden, 10-12 minutes. Serve warm and top with vanilla ice cream if desired.

Lemon & Honey Pear Chips

Serves: 1 | Total Time: 30 minutes

Ingredients

2 firm pears, thinly sliced

1 tablespoon lemon juice

½ teaspoon ground cinnamon

1 teaspoon honey

Directions

Start by preheating your air fryer to 380°F. Arrange the pear slices on the parchment-lined cooking basket. Drizzle with lemon juice and honey and sprinkle with cinnamon. Air Fry for 6-8 minutes, shaking the basket once, until golden. Leave to cool. Serve immediately or save for later in an airtight container. Good for 2 days.

CHICKEN RECIPES

Buffalo Hot Chicken Wings

Serves: 1 | Total Time: 35 minutes

Ingredients

4-6 chicken wings, split at the joint
½ tablespoon butter, softened
2 tablespoons buffalo wing sauce

Salt and black pepper to taste
¼ teaspoon red chili powder
¼ teaspoon garlic-ginger puree

Directions

Preheat the air fryer to 400°F. Sprinkle the chicken wings with salt, pepper, red chili powder, grated garlic, and ginger. Place the seasoned chicken wings in the greased frying basket and Air Fry for 12 minutes, tossing once.

While the wings are cooking, whisk together the butter and buffalo sauce in a bowl. After the initial 12 minutes, shake the basket and Air Fry for 10 minutes.

Once done, transfer the hot wings into the bowl with the buffalo sauce. Toss until the wings are evenly coated. Serve immediately and enjoy your delicious chicken wings!

Corn-Coated Chicken Goujons

Serves 1 | Total Time: 25 minutes

Ingredients

5 ounces chicken breast, cut into strips
¼ cup lightly crushed corn crackers
1 tbsp flour

1 tsp olive oil
¼ tsp lime pepper seasoning
1 egg white, beaten

Directions

Preheat your air fryer to 380°F. Season the chicken strips with lime pepper seasoning, then dust them in the flour. Next, dip in the egg whites and coat in the corn crackers. Put onto the greased frying basket. Air Fry for 10-14 minutes, turning halfway through, until golden and crisp.

French-Style Chicken Wings

Serves: 1 | Total Time: 35 minutes

Ingredients

4-6 chicken wings, split at the joint
½ tablespoon water
Salt and black pepper to taste
¼ teaspoon red chili powder

½ tablespoon butter, melted
¼ tablespoon Dijon mustard
½ tablespoon honey
½ teaspoon apple cider vinegar

Directions

Preheat the air fryer to 250°F. Pour water into the bottom of the frying basket to minimize smoke from fat drippings. Sprinkle the chicken wings with salt, pepper, and red chili powder. Place the seasoned chicken wings in the greased frying basket and Air Fry for 12 minutes, tossing once.

While the wings cook, whisk together melted butter, Dijon mustard, honey, apple cider vinegar, and salt in a bowl. After the initial 12 minutes, shake the basket and Air Fry for 10 minutes.

Once done, transfer the hot wings into the bowl with the mustard sauce. Toss until the wings are evenly coated. Serve immediately and savor the delightful flavor of your mustard chicken wings!

Lemony & Sweet Chicken Wings

Serves: 1 | Total Time: 30 minutes

Ingredients

4-6 chicken wings
Salt and black pepper to taste
1 tablespoon honey
½ tablespoon lemon juice
1 tablespoon chicken stock

1 garlic clove, minced
1 thinly sliced green onion
2 tablespoons barbecue sauce
½ tablespoon sesame seeds

Directions

Start by preheating your air fryer to 390°F. Season the wings with salt and pepper and place them in the frying basket. Air Fry for 20 minutes.

Shake the basket a couple of times during cooking. In a bowl, mix the honey, lemon juice, chicken stock, and garlic. Take the wings out of the fryer and place them in a baking pan.

Add the sauce and toss, coating completely. Put the pan in the air fryer and Air Fry for 4-5 minutes until golden and cooked through, with no pink showing. Top with green onions and sesame seeds, then serve with BBQ sauce.

Buttery Chicken Thighs

Serves: 1 | Total Time: 25 minutes

Ingredients

2 bone-in chicken thighs, skinless
½ tablespoon butter, melted
¼ teaspoon garlic powder

¼ teaspoon lemon zest
Salt and black pepper to taste
2 lemon slices

Directions

Preheat the air fryer to 380°F. Rub the chicken thighs with melted butter, lemon zest, garlic powder, and salt. Place the chicken thighs in one piece of foil and sprinkle with black pepper. Top with slices of lemon. Bake in the air fryer for 20-22 minutes until the chicken thighs are golden. Serve your chicken thighs hot and savor the zesty goodness!

Mexican-Style Chicken Nachos

Serves: 1 | Total Time: 15 minutes

Ingredients

1 tablespoon baked corn tortilla chips
½ cup leftover roast chicken, shredded
¼ cup canned black beans
½ red bell pepper, chopped

¼ grated carrot
¼ jalapeño pepper, minced
1 tablespoon grated Swiss cheese
½ tomato, chopped

Directions

Preheat your air fryer to 360°F. Lay the tortilla chips in a single layer in the air fryer basket. Add the shredded chicken, black beans, bell pepper, carrot, and jalapeño pepper, and sprinkle the Swiss cheese on the chips. Air fry for 7-10 minutes, ensuring the cheese melts and gets slightly browned.

Once done, remove the nachos from the air fryer and transfer them to a serving plate. Garnish with chopped tomatoes. Serve immediately!

Shredded Chicken Frittata Cups

Serves: 1 | Total Time: 15 minutes

Ingredients

2 tablespoons shredded cooked chicken breasts
2 eggs
1 tablespoon heavy cream

1 teaspoon Tabasco sauce
1 tablespoon grated Asiago cheese
1 tablespoon chives, chopped

Directions

Preheat the air fryer to 350°F. Mix eggs, heavy cream, Tabasco sauce, grated Asiago cheese, chives, and shredded chicken in a bowl.

Grease 2 muffin cups and evenly divide the egg mixture between them. Place the muffin cups in the air fryer basket. Air fry for 8-10 minutes or until the frittata cups are set. Allow them to cool slightly before serving. Enjoy!

Greek-Style Chicken Wings

Serves: 1 | Total Time: 30 minutes

Ingredients

4-6 chicken wings
¼ tablespoon chili sauce
¼ teaspoon dried oregano
¼ teaspoon smoked paprika
¼ teaspoon garlic powder
Salt to taste

1 tablespoon Greek yogurt
½ tablespoon mayonnaise
¼ tablespoon lemon juice
1 tablespoon chopped parsley
½ cucumber, cut into sticks
½ carrot, cut into sticks

Directions

Add the chicken wings, chili sauce, oregano, garlic powder, smoked paprika, and salt in a large bowl. Toss to coat well, then set aside.

In a small bowl, mix mayonnaise and Greek yogurt. Stir in lemon juice and parsley until blended. Refrigerate covered until it is time to serve.

Preheat the air fryer to 390°F. Place the seasoned chicken in the greased frying basket and Air Fry for 15-20 minutes, flipping the chicken once, until crispy and browned.

While the chicken is cooking, prepare cucumber and carrot sticks. Once done, serve the Greek-style chicken wings with cucumber, carrot sticks, and the refreshing yogurt dip. Enjoy your delightful chicken wings!

Air Fried Flatbread Pizza

Serves: 1 | Total Time: 15 minutes

Ingredients

½ cup cooked chicken breast, cubed

2 tablespoons grated mozzarella cheese

1 flatbread

2 tablespoons olive oil

2 garlic cloves, minced

½ teaspoon red pepper flakes

1 cup kale

½ sliced red onion

Directions

Preheat the air fryer to 380°F. Lightly brush the top of the flatbread with olive oil. Top with the minced garlic, red pepper flakes, kale, sliced red onion, cubed chicken, and mozzarella cheese.

Place the resulting pizza into the frying basket. Air fry for 6-8 minutes or until the edges are crispy and the cheese is melted and bubbly. Serve immediately and enjoy the flavorful combination of ingredients!

Chicken Strips with Parmesan

Serves: 1 | Total Time: 40 minutes

Ingredients

1 chicken breast, sliced into strips

1 tablespoon grated Parmesan cheese

¼ cup breadcrumbs

¼ tablespoon chicken seasoning

1 small egg, beaten

Salt and black pepper to taste

Directions

Start by preheating your air fryer to 350°F. Mix the breadcrumbs, Parmesan cheese, chicken seasoning, salt, and pepper in a mixing bowl. Coat the chicken with the crumb mixture. Dip in the beaten eggs. Finally, coat again with the dry ingredients.

Arrange the coated chicken pieces on the greased frying basket and Air Fry for 15 minutes. Turn over halfway through cooking and cook for another 15 minutes. Serve immediately.

Kale & Rice Chicken Rolls

Serves: 1 | Total Time: 35 minutes

Ingredients

2 boneless, skinless chicken thighs

¼ teaspoon ground fenugreek seeds

½ cup cooked wild rice

1 sundried tomato, diced

¼ cup chopped kale

1 garlic clove, minced

½ teaspoon salt

½ lemon, juiced

¼ cup crumbled feta

½ tablespoon olive oil

Directions

Preheat the air fryer to 380°F. Place each chicken thigh between two pieces of plastic wrap and pound them out to about ¼-inch thick using a meat mallet or a rolling pin.

In a bowl, combine cooked wild rice, diced sundried tomato, chopped kale, minced garlic, salt, fenugreek seeds, and lemon juice. Mix well.

Divide the rice mixture among the chicken thighs and sprinkle with crumbled feta.

Fold the sides of the chicken thigh over the filling and gently place each one seam-side down into the greased air frying basket. Drizzle the stuffed chicken thighs with olive oil.

Roast the stuffed chicken thighs for 12 minutes, then turn them over and cook for an additional 10 minutes or until the chicken is cooked through and golden. Serve and enjoy!

Homestyle Chicken Skewers

Serves: 1 | Total Time: 30 minutes + marinating time

Ingredients

½ pound boneless, skinless chicken thighs, cut into pieces

¼ sweet onion, cut into 1-inch pieces

¼ zucchini, cut into 1-inch pieces

¼ red bell pepper, cut into 1-inch pieces

1 tablespoon olive oil

¼ teaspoon garlic powder

¼ teaspoon shallot powder

¼ teaspoon ground cumin

¼ teaspoon dried oregano

¼ teaspoon dried thyme

1 tablespoon lemon juice

¼ tablespoon apple cider vinegar

1 grape tomato

Directions

Combine olive oil, garlic powder, shallot powder, cumin, oregano, thyme, lemon juice, and vinegar in a bowl. Mix well. Alternate skewering the chicken, bell pepper, onion, zucchini, and tomatoes.

Place the prepared skewers in a greased baking dish and pour the olive oil marinade over the top. Turn to coat. Cover with plastic wrap and refrigerate for the recommended marinating time.

Preheat the air fryer to 380°F. Remove the skewers from the marinade and arrange them in a single layer on the frying basket. Bake for 14-16 minutes, rotating once for even cooking. Let the skewers sit for 5 minutes before serving. Enjoy the tasty and flavorful combination!

Asian Chicken Bulgogi

Serves: 1 | Total Time: 30 minutes

Ingredients

2 boneless, skinless chicken thighs, cubed

1 scallion, sliced, whites and green separated

1 tablespoon grated carrots

2 tablespoons rice vinegar

¼ teaspoon granulated sugar

Salt to taste

¼ tablespoon tamari

1 teaspoon sesame oil

¼ tablespoon light brown sugar

¼ tablespoon lime juice

¼ tablespoon soy sauce

1 clove garlic, minced

¼ Asian pear

½ teaspoon minced ginger

½ cups cooked white rice

½ teaspoon sesame seeds

Directions

In a bowl, combine the carrots, half of the rice vinegar, sugar, and salt. Let it chill covered in the fridge until ready to use. Mix tamari, sesame oil, soy sauce, brown sugar, remaining rice vinegar, lime juice, garlic, Asian pear, ginger, and scallion whites in a bowl. Toss in chicken thighs and let them marinate for 10 minutes.

Preheat the air fryer to 350°F. Using a slotted spoon, transfer chicken thighs to the frying basket, reserving the marinade. Air Fry for 10-12 minutes, shaking once.

Place chicken over a bed of rice on serving plates and scatter with scallion greens and sesame seeds. Serve with pickled carrots for a delicious and flavorful meal!

Italian Chicken Parmigiana

Serves: 1 | Total Time: 30 minutes

Ingredients

1 chicken breast

1 cup breadcrumbs

2 eggs, beaten

Salt and black pepper to taste

1 tablespoon dried basil

1 cup passata

2 provolone cheese slices

1 tablespoon Parmesan cheese

Directions

Start by preheating your air fryer to 350°F. Mix the breadcrumbs, basil, salt, and pepper in a mixing bowl. Coat the chicken breast with the crumb mixture, then dip in the beaten eggs. Finally, coat again with the dry ingredients.

Place the coated chicken breast on the greased frying basket and Air Fry for 14-16 minutes. At the 8-minutes mark, turn the breast over and cook for the remaining 10 minutes. Pour half of the passata into a baking pan. When the chicken is ready, remove it to the passata-covered pan.

Pour the remaining passata over the fried chicken and arrange the provolone cheese slices on top and sprinkle with Parmesan cheese. Bake for 5 minutes until the chicken is crisped and the cheese melted and lightly toasted. Serve your delicious chicken, and enjoy the classic Italian flavors!

Sweet & Spicy Chicken Wings

Serves: 1 | Total Time: 25 minutes

Ingredients

½ pound chicken wings

½ tablespoon olive oil

½ tablespoon brown sugar

½ tablespoon maple syrup

1 teaspoon apple cider vinegar

¼ teaspoon Aleppo pepper flakes

Salt to taste

Directions

Preheat the air fryer to 390°F. Toss the wings with olive oil in a bowl. Bake the wings in the air fryer for 15 minutes, shaking the basket once or twice.

While the chicken is cooking, whisk together brown sugar, maple syrup, apple cider vinegar, Aleppo pepper flakes, and salt in a small bowl. After 15 minutes, transfer the wings to a baking pan and pour the sauce over them. Toss well to coat.

Place the baking pan back into the air fryer and cook for 5 minutes or until the wings are glazed. Serve hot and savor the perfect blend of spicy and sweet flavors!

Cajun Chicken Legs

Serves: 1 | Total Time: 35 minutes

Ingredients

1 teaspoon Cajun seasoning

¼ teaspoon mango powder

2 chicken legs, bone-in

Directions

Preheat your air fryer to 360°F. In a bowl, mix half of the Cajun seasoning with 2 tablespoons of water, stirring well to dissolve any lumps. In a shallow bowl, combine the remaining Cajun seasoning and mango powder. Dip each chicken leg into the batter and coat it in the mango seasoning.

Lightly spritz the chicken with cooking spray. Place the chicken in the air fryer and Air Fry for 14-16 minutes, turning once, until the chicken is cooked through, and the coating is brown and crispy. Serve your chicken legs hot and savor the spicy goodness!

Smoky Chicken Drumettes

Serves: 1 | Total Time: 30 minutes + marinating time

Ingredients

2 chicken drumettes

½ cup buttermilk

2 tablespoons bread crumbs

¼ teaspoon smoked paprika

¼ teaspoon chicken seasoning

¼ teaspoon garlic powder

Salt and black pepper to taste

1 teaspoon lemon juice

Directions

Mix drumettes and buttermilk in a bowl and let sit covered in the fridge overnight.

Preheat your air fryer to 350°F. In a shallow bowl, combine the remaining ingredients. Shake excess buttermilk off drumettes and dip them in the breadcrumb mixture. Place breaded drumettes in the greased frying basket and Air Fry for 12 minutes.

Increase air fryer temperature to 400°F, toss the chicken, and cook for 8 minutes. Let rest for 5 minutes before serving.

Piri Piri Chicken Drumettes

Serves: 1 | Total Time: 25 minutes

Ingredients

¼ cup crushed cracker crumbs

¼ tablespoon sweet paprika

¼ tablespoon smoked paprika

¼ tablespoon Piri Piri seasoning

¼ teaspoon sea salt

½ teaspoon onion powder

¼ teaspoon garlic powder

2 chicken drumettes

½ tablespoon olive oil

Directions

Preheat the air fryer to 380°F. Combine the cracker crumbs, sweet paprika, smoked paprika, Piri Piri seasoning, sea salt, onion powder, and garlic powder in a bowl. Mix well and set aside.

Put the chicken in a large bowl, drizzle with olive oil, and toss to coat. Sprinkle the breading mix over the drumettes and press the mix into the chicken. Place the drumettes in the frying basket.

Air Fry for 10-12 minutes, shaking the basket once, until the drumettes are golden and crisp. Serve chicken drumettes hot and enjoy the flavorful crunch!

Mediterranean Chicken Salad

Serves: 1 | Total Time: 25 minutes

Ingredients

2 tablespoons honey-mustard salad dressing

1 chicken breast, cubed

½ red onion, sliced

½ orange bell pepper, sliced

½ cup sliced zucchini

¼ teaspoon dried thyme

¼ cup mayonnaise

1 tablespoon lemon juice

Directions

Preheat the air fryer to 400°F. Add chicken, onion, pepper, and zucchini to the fryer. Drizzle with 1 tablespoon of the salad dressing and sprinkle with thyme. Toss to coat. Bake for 5-6 minutes.

Shake the basket, then continue cooking for another 5-6 minutes. In a bowl, combine the rest of the dressing, mayonnaise, and lemon juice. Transfer the chicken and vegetables and toss to coat. Serve and enjoy!

Tzatziki Chicken with Rice

Serves: 1 | Total Time: 25 minutes

Ingredients

1 chicken breast, cubed

1 tablespoon cream cheese

1 teaspoon olive oil

¼ teaspoon dried oregano

¼ teaspoon ground cumin

¼ teaspoon ground cinnamon

¼ teaspoon ground nutmeg

Salt and black pepper to taste

¼ teaspoon ground turmeric

½ cup cooked rice

¼ cup Tzatziki sauce

Directions

Preheat the air fryer to 380°F. In a bowl, mix together chicken breast, cream cheese, olive oil, dried oregano, ground cumin, ground cinnamon, ground nutmeg, salt, pepper, and ground turmeric until the chicken is well-coated.

Spread the chicken mixture in the frying basket. Bake for 10 minutes. Stir the chicken mixture and bake for an additional 5 minutes or until the chicken is cooked through. Serve your chicken gyros with over cooked rice and drizzle with Tzatziki sauce. Enjoy!

Famous Barberton Chicken

Serves: 1 | Total Time: 20 minutes

Ingredients

½ tablespoon melted lard

1 chicken breast

2 tablespoons bread crumbs

2 tablespoons flour

1 small egg, beaten

Directions

Preheat the air fryer to 350°F. Roll chicken in flour. Dip in beaten egg, then coat in bread crumbs, pressing crumbs into chicken; gently shake off excess. Brush with melted lard. Air Fry for 14-16 minutes until golden brown. Serve your chicken breast hot and enjoy!

Chorizo Chicken Empanadas

Serves: 1 | Total Time: 25 minutes

Ingredients

1 chorizo sausage, casings removed and crumbled

½ tablespoon olive oil

¼ chicken breast, diced

3 black olives, sliced

¼ teaspoon chili powder

¼ teaspoon paprika

½ tablespoon raisins

2 empanada shells

Directions

Preheat the air fryer to 350°F. Warm the oil in a skillet over medium heat. Sauté the chicken and chorizo, breaking up the chorizo, for 3-4 minutes. Add the raisins, chili powder, paprika, and olives. Stir and kill the heat, letting the mixture cool slightly.

Divide the chorizo mixture between the empanada shells and fold them over to cover the filling. Seal the edges with water and press down with a fork to secure. Place the empanadas in the air fryer basket. Bake for 15 minutes, flipping once, until they are golden and crispy. Serve and enjoy!

Easy Chicken Hoagies

Serves: 1 | Total Time: 30 minutes

Ingredients

¼ cup button mushrooms, sliced

1 hoagie bun, halved

½ chicken breast, cubed

¼ white onion, sliced

½ cup bell pepper strips

1 cheddar cheese slice

Directions

Start by preheating your air fryer to 320°F. Place the chicken pieces, onions, bell pepper strips, and mushroom slices on one side of the frying basket. Lay the hoagie bun halves, crusty side up and soft side down, on the other half of the air fryer. Bake for 10 minutes. Flip the hoagie buns and cover with cheddar cheese.

Stir the chicken and vegetables. Cook for another 6 minutes until the cheese is melted and the chicken is juicy on the inside and crispy on the outside. Place the cheesy hoagie halves on a serving plate and cover one half with the chicken and veggies. Close with the other cheesy hoagie half.

Indian-Style Chicken Salad

Serves: 1 | Total Time: 30 minutes

Ingredients

1 teaspoon chopped golden raisins

½ Granny Smith apple, grated

1 chicken breast

Salt and black pepper to taste

2 tablespoons mayonnaise

½ tablespoon lime juice

¼ teaspoon curry powder

½ sliced avocado

1 scallion, minced

1 teaspoon chopped pecans

¼ teaspoon poppy seeds

Directions

Preheat your air fryer to 350°F. Sprinkle chicken breast with salt and pepper, place it in the greased frying basket, and Air Fry for 8-10 minutes, tossing once. Let rest for 5 minutes before cutting.

In a salad bowl, combine chopped chicken, mayonnaise, lime juice, curry powder, raisins, apple, avocado, scallion, and pecans. Let sit covered in the fridge until ready to eat. Before serving, sprinkle with poppy seeds. Enjoy!

Yogurt-Marinated Chicken Legs

Serves: 1 | Total Time: 30 minutes + marinating time

Ingredients

½ cup Greek yogurt

½ tablespoon Dijon mustard

¼ teaspoon smoked paprika

¼ tablespoon crushed red pepper

¼ teaspoon garlic powder

¼ teaspoon dried oregano

¼ teaspoon dried thyme

¼ teaspoon ground cumin

1 tablespoon lemon juice

Salt and black pepper to taste

2 chicken legs

1 tablespoon butter, melted

Directions

Combine all ingredients, except chicken and butter, in a bowl. Fold in chicken legs and toss until coated. Let it sit covered in the fridge for 60 minutes up to overnight.

Preheat the air fryer to 375°F. Shake excess marinade from chicken, place them in the greased frying basket, and Air Fry for 18 minutes. Brush melted butter and flip once during cooking. Let the chicken chill for 5 minutes before serving. Enjoy!

Mayo & Mustard Chicken Bites

Serves: 1 | Total Time: 20 minutes + chilling time

Ingredients

1 tablespoon horseradish mustard

½ tablespoon mayonnaise

½ tablespoon olive oil

1 chicken breast, cubes

½ tablespoon parsley

Directions

Combine all ingredients, excluding parsley, in a bowl. Let it marinate covered in the fridge for 30 minutes.

Preheat the air fryer to 350°F. Place chicken cubes in the greased frying basket. Air Fry for 9 minutes, tossing once. Serve your chicken bites immediately, sprinkled with parsley. Enjoy the zesty goodness!

Chicken Salad with White Dressing

Serves: 1 | Total Time: 20 minutes

Ingredients

1 chicken breast, cut into strips

¼ cup diced peeled red onion

½ peeled English cucumber, diced

¼ tablespoon crushed red pepper flakes

½ cup Greek yogurt

1 tablespoon light mayonnaise

¼ tablespoon mustard

¼ teaspoon chopped dill

¼ teaspoon chopped mint

¼ teaspoon lemon juice

1 garlic clove, minced

Salt and black pepper to taste

1 cup mixed greens

2 Kalamata olives, halved

½ tomato, diced

2 tablespoons feta cheese crumbles

Directions

In a small bowl, whisk the Greek yogurt, mayonnaise, mustard, cucumber, dill, mint, salt, lemon juice, and garlic, and let chill the resulting dressing covered in the fridge until ready to use. Sprinkle the chicken strips with salt and pepper.

Preheat your air fryer to 350°F. Place them in the greased frying basket and Air Fry for 10 minutes, tossing once. Place the mixed greens and pepper flakes in a salad bowl. Top each with red onion, olives, tomato, feta cheese, and grilled chicken. Drizzle with the dressing and serve.

Masala Chicken Tandoori

Serves: 1 | Total Time: 35 minutes + marinating time

Ingredients

1 chicken breast, cubed

¼ cup hung curd

¼ teaspoon turmeric powder

¼ teaspoon red chili powder

¼ teaspoon chaat masala powder

Pinch of salt

Directions

Start by preheating your air fryer to 350°F. Mix the hung curd, turmeric, red chili powder, chaat masala powder, and salt in a mixing bowl. Stir until the mixture is free of lumps. Coat the chicken with the mixture, cover, and refrigerate for 30 minutes to marinate.

Place the marinated chicken chunks in a baking pan and drizzle with the remaining marinade. Bake for 25 minutes until the chicken is juicy and spiced. Serve warm.

Adobo Chicken Roulades

Serves: 1 | Total Time: 35 minutes

Ingredients

¼ green bell pepper, cut into strips

½ carrot, cut into strips

2 chicken breast halves

¼ lime, juiced

1 tablespoon adobo seasoning

½ spring onion, thinly sliced

Directions

Preheat your air fryer to 400°F. Place the breast halves between two plastic wraps and gently pound with a rolling pin to ¼-inch thickness. Drizzle with lime juice and season with adobo seasoning.

Divide the carrot, green pepper, and spring onion equally between the 2 breast halves. Roll up each chicken breast and secure with toothpicks. Place the roulades in the frying basket and lightly spray with cooking oil. Bake for 12 minutes, turning once. Serve warm.

Middle Eastern Chicken Drumsticks

Serves: 1 | Total Time: 30 minutes

Ingredients

½ tablespoon butter, melted

2 chicken drumsticks

¼ tablespoon Za'atar seasoning

Salt and black pepper to taste

¼ lemon, zested

1 tablespoon parsley, chopped

Directions

Preheat the air fryer to 390°F. In a bowl, mix the Za'atar seasoning, lemon zest, parsley, salt, and pepper. Add the chicken drumsticks and toss to coat.

Place the drumsticks in the air fryer basket and brush them with melted butter. Air Fry for 18-20 minutes, flipping once, until they are crispy. Serve and enjoy!

Hot Tabasco Chicken Wings

Serves: 1 | Total Time: 40 minutes

Ingredients

4-6 chicken wings

¼ cup melted butter

1 teaspoon Tabasco sauce

¼ tablespoon lemon juice

¼ tablespoon Worcestershire sauce

¼ teaspoon cayenne pepper

¼ teaspoon garlic powder

¼ teaspoon lemon zest

¼ teaspoon adobo seasoning

Salt and black pepper to taste

Directions

Start by preheating your air fryer to 350°F. Place the melted butter, Tabasco sauce, lemon juice, Worcestershire sauce, cayenne pepper, garlic, lemon zest, adobo seasoning, salt, and pepper in a bowl and stir to combine.

Dip the chicken wings into the mixture, coating thoroughly. Lay the coated chicken wings on the foil-lined frying basket in an even layer. Air Fry for 16-18 minutes. Shake the basket several times during cooking until the chicken wings are crispy brown.

Marinara Chicken Pizzadilla

Serves: 1 | Total Time: 25 minutes

Ingredients

1 cup cooked boneless, skinless chicken, shredded

¼ cup grated provolone cheese

2 basil and mint leaves, julienned

Salt to taste

¼ teaspoon garlic powder

1 teaspoon butter, melted

2 small flour tortillas

¼ cup marinara sauce

¼ cup grated cheddar cheese

Directions

Preheat your air fryer to 360°F. Sprinkle the chicken with salt and garlic powder. Brush one side of a tortilla lightly with melted butter. Spread it with marinara sauce, then it top with chicken, cheddar cheese, provolone, and finally, the basil and mint leaves.

Top with the second tortilla and lightly brush the top with butter. Put the quesadilla, butter side down, in the fryer and Bake for 3 minutes. Cut them into 2 sections to serve.

Korean-Style Chicken Legs

Serves: 1 | Total Time: 30 minutes + chilling time

Ingredients

1 scallion, sliced, whites and greens separated
1 teaspoon tamari
1 tablespoon sesame oil
¼ teaspoon sesame seeds
1 teaspoon honey
¼ tablespoon gochujang

¼ tablespoon ketchup
1 garlic clove, minced
¼ teaspoon ground ginger
Salt and black pepper to taste
2 chicken legs
½ tablespoon parsley

Directions

Whisk all ingredients, except chicken and scallion greens, in a bowl. Reserve 1 tablespoon of marinade. Toss chicken legs in the remaining marinade and chill for 30 minutes.

Preheat the air fryer to 400°F. Place chicken legs in the greased frying basket and Air Fry for 10 minutes. Turn the chicken and cook for 8 more minutes.

Let the cooked chicken sit in a serving dish for 5 minutes. Coat the cooked chicken with the reserved marinade and scatter with scallion greens, sesame seeds, and parsley to serve.

Yummy Chicken Fingers

Serves: 1 | Total Time: 30 minutes

Ingredients

¼ pound chicken breast fingers
¼ tablespoon chicken seasoning
¼ teaspoon mustard powder

Salt and black pepper to taste
1 egg
1 tablespoon bread crumbs

Directions

Preheat the air fryer to 400°F. In a bowl, combine the chicken fingers with chicken seasoning, mustard powder, salt, and pepper; mix well.

Set up two small bowls. In one bowl, beat the egg. In the second bowl, add the bread crumbs. Dip each chicken finger in the egg, then dredge in breadcrumbs. Place the chicken fingers in the air fryer. Lightly spray with cooking oil. Air Fry for 8 minutes, shaking the basket once, until the chicken fingers are crispy and cooked through. Serve warm and enjoy your delicious chicken fingers!

Tex-Mex Chicken Drumsticks

Serves: 1 | Total Time: 40 minutes

Ingredients

¼ can chipotle chilies packed in adobo sauce

1 teaspoon grated Mexican cheese

2 chicken drumsticks

1 small egg, beaten

2 tablespoons bread crumbs

½ tablespoon cornflakes

Salt and black pepper to taste

Directions

Preheat the air fryer to 350°F. Place the chilies in the adobo sauce in your blender and pulse until a fine paste is formed. Transfer to a bowl and add the beaten egg. Combine thoroughly. Mix the breadcrumbs, Mexican cheese, cornflakes, salt, and pepper in a separate bowl and set aside.

Coat the chicken drumsticks with the crumb mixture, then dip into the bowl with wet ingredients, then dip again into the dry ingredients. Arrange the chicken drumsticks on the greased frying basket in a single flat layer. Air Fry for 14-16 minutes, turning each chicken drumstick over once. Serve your chicken drumsticks warm, with a deliciously spicy kick!

Chicken Thighs with Salsa Verde

Serves: 1 | Total Time: 35 minutes

Ingredients

2 boneless, skinless chicken thighs

½ cup salsa verde

1 mashed garlic clove

Directions

Preheat the air fryer to 350°F. Add chicken thighs to a small baking dish and cover with salsa verde and mashed garlic. Place the baking dish in the greased frying basket. Air Fry for 30 minutes. Let the chicken thighs rest for 5 minutes before serving.

Classic Cobb Salad

Serves: 1 | Total Time: 30 minutes

Ingredients

1 cooked bacon slice, crumbled

¼ cup diced red onion

1 oz crumbled Stilton cheese

Salt and black pepper to taste

1 teaspoon olive oil

1 teaspoon apple cider vinegar

1 chicken breast

1 cup torn iceberg lettuce

1 cup baby spinach

¼ cup ranch dressing

½ avocado, diced

½ beefsteak tomato, diced

1 hard-boiled egg, diced

1 tablespoon parsley

Directions

Start by preheating your air fryer to 350°F. Cover the chicken with plastic wraps and pound it with a meat tenderizer to ½-inch thickness. Season with salt and pepper and rub with olive oil. Place chicken breast in the frying basket. Air Fry for 14-16 minutes, flipping them halfway through the cooking.

Let it cool, then chop it into bite-sized pieces. Combine the lettuce, baby spinach, parsley, and half of the ranch dressing on a salad plate and toss to coat.

Arrange the cooked chicken and the remaining ingredients in rows over the greens. Drizzle with the remaining ranch dressing. Serve.

Weeknight Chicken Strips

Serves: 1 | Total Time: 20 minutes

Ingredients

½ pound chicken strips
½ cup sweet chili sauce

¼ cup bread crumbs
¼ cup cornmeal

Directions

Start by preheating your air fryer to 350°F. Combine chicken strips and sweet chili sauce in a bowl until fully coated. In another bowl, mix the remaining ingredients.

Dredge strips in the mixture. Shake off any excess. Place chicken strips in the greased frying basket and Air Fry for 10 minutes, tossing once. Serve right away.

Tasty Satay Chicken Skewers

Serves: 1 | Total Time: 30 minutes + marinating time

Ingredients

½ chicken breast, cut into strips
½ tablespoon Thai red curry paste
1 tablespoon peanut butter
¼ tablespoon maple syrup
¼ tablespoon tamari
¼ tablespoon lime juice

1 teaspoon chopped onions
¼ teaspoon minced ginger
½ garlic clove, minced
¼ cup coconut milk
¼ teaspoon fish sauce
½ tablespoon chopped cilantro

Directions

Mix the peanut butter, maple syrup, tamari, lime juice, tamari, onions, ginger, garlic, and ½ tablespoon of water in a bowl. Reserve 1 tablespoon of the sauce. Set aside.

Combine the reserved peanut sauce, fish sauce, coconut milk, Thai red curry paste, cilantro, and chicken strips in a bowl. Let it marinate in the fridge for 15 minutes.

Preheat the air fryer to 350°F. Thread chicken strips onto skewers and place them on a kebab rack. Place the rack in the greased frying basket. Air Fry for 12 minutes. Serve your chicken skewers with the previously prepared peanut sauce on the side. Enjoy the flavorful bites!

The Complete Club Sandwiches

Serves: 1 | Total Time: 50 minutes

Ingredients

¼ cup buttermilk

1 small egg

¼ cup bread crumbs

¼ teaspoon garlic powder

Salt and black pepper to taste

1 chicken cutlet

½ tablespoon butter, melted

1 hamburger bun

1 tablespoon mayonnaise

1 teaspoon yellow mustard

2 dill pickle chips

1 iceberg lettuce leaf

¼ sliced avocado

1 cooked bacon slice

2 vine-ripe tomato slices

Directions

Preheat the air fryer to 400°F. Beat the buttermilk and egg in a bowl. In another bowl, combine breadcrumbs, garlic powder, salt, and black pepper. Dip chicken cutlets in the egg mixture, then dredge them in the breadcrumbs mixture.

Brush chicken cutlet lightly with melted butter on both sides, place it in the greased frying basket, and Air Fry for 18-20 minutes. Spread the mayonnaise on the top bun and mustard on the bottom bun.

Add chicken onto bottom bun and top with pickles, lettuce, avocado, bacon, and tomato. Cover with the top bun. Serve your chicken sandwich and enjoy this classic, hearty meal!

Chili Chicken Tortillas

Serves: 1 | Total Time: 35 minutes

Ingredients

½ cup cooked chicken breasts, shredded

¼ (7-oz) can diced green chilies, including juice

1 cup grated Mexican cheese blend

½ tablespoon sour cream

¼ teaspoon chili powder

¼ teaspoon cumin

¼ tablespoon chipotle sauce

¼ teaspoon dried onion flakes

Salt to taste

1 tablespoon butter, melted

2 flour tortillas

Directions

In a small bowl, whisk together the sour cream, chipotle sauce, and chili powder. Let it chill in the fridge until ready to use.

Preheat the air fryer to 350°F. In a bowl, mix the chicken, green chilies, cumin, and salt. Set aside. Brush one side of two tortilla lightly with melted butter. Layer with chicken, dried onion flakes, and Mexican cheese. Top with remaining tortillas and lightly brush the top with butter.

Transfer the quesadillas, butter side down, to the air fryer basket. Air Fry for 3 minutes until they are crispy and the cheese is melted. Serve with cream sauce on the side. Enjoy!

Pesto Chicken Caprese

Serves: 1 | Total Time: 30 minutes

Ingredients

½ tablespoon grated Parmesan cheese

2 fresh mozzarella cheese slices

1 grape tomato, halved

1 garlic clove, minced

½ teaspoon olive oil

Salt and black pepper to taste

1 chicken cutlet

¼ tablespoon prepared pesto

1 small egg, beaten

2 teaspoons bread crumbs

¼ tablespoon Italian seasoning

¼ teaspoon balsamic vinegar

1 tablespoon chopped fresh basil

Directions

Preheat the air fryer to 400°F. In a bowl, coat the tomatoes with garlic, olive oil, salt, and pepper. Air Fry for 5 minutes, shaking them twice. Set aside when soft.

Place the cutlet between two sheets of parchment paper. Pound the chicken to ¼-inch thickness using a meat mallet. Season on both sides with salt and pepper. Spread an even coat of pesto.

Put the beaten egg in a shallow bowl. Mix the crumbs, Italian seasoning, and Parmesan in a second shallow bowl. Dip the chicken in the egg bowl and then in the crumb mix. Press the crumbs so that they stick to the chicken.

Place the chicken in the greased frying basket. Air Fry the chicken for 6-8 minutes, flipping once until golden and cooked through.

Put the mozzarella cheese and tomato on top. Return it to the frying basket and melt the cheese for 2 minutes. Remove from the fryer, drizzle with balsamic vinegar, and sprinkle basil on top.

Herby Chicken Breast

Serves: 1 | Total Time: 30 minutes

Ingredients

½ tablespoon olive oil

½ tablespoon balsamic vinegar

1 garlic clove, minced

½ tomato, diced

½ tablespoon Italian seasoning

½ tablespoon chopped fresh basil

½ teaspoon thyme, chopped

1 chicken breast

Directions

Start by preheating your air fryer to 370°F. Combine the olive oil, balsamic vinegar, garlic, thyme, tomato, Italian seasoning, and basil in a medium bowl. Set aside. Cut 4-5 slits into the chicken breast ¾ of the way through.

Place the chicken with the slits facing up, in the greased frying basket. Bake for 7 minutes. Spoon the bruschetta mixture into the slits of the chicken. Cook for another 3 minutes. Allow chicken to sit and cool for a few minutes. Serve and enjoy!

Easy Taco Chicken

Serves: 1 | Total Time: 35 minutes

Ingredients

½ chicken breast

¼ tablespoon Ranch seasoning

¼ tablespoon taco seasoning

1 tablespoon flour

1 small egg (whisked)

1 tablespoon bread crumbs

2 small flour tortillas

¼ cup shredded lettuce

1 tablespoon ranch dressing

½ tablespoon fresh cilantro, chopped

Directions

Start by preheating your air fryer to 370°F. Rub the chicken breast with ranch and taco seasonings. In one shallow bowl, add flour. In another shallow bowl, beat the egg. In the third shallow bowl, add bread crumbs. Lightly spray the air fryer basket with cooking oil.

First, dip the chicken in the flour, dredge in egg, and then finish by coating with bread crumbs. Place it in the fryer and Bake for 6-8 minutes. Flip and cook further for 4 minutes until crisp.

Allow the chicken to cool for a few minutes, then cut into strips. Serve with shredded lettuce, ranch dressing, cilantro and tortillas. Enjoy!

Moroccan Chicken Wings

Serves: 1 | Total Time: 25 minutes

Ingredients

4 whole chicken wings

¼ teaspoon garlic powder

¼ teaspoon dried oregano

¼ tablespoon harissa seasoning

Directions

Start by preheating your air fryer to 400°F. Season the wings with garlic, harissa seasoning, and oregano. Place them in the greased frying basket and spray with cooking oil spray. Air Fry for 10 minutes, shake the basket, and cook for another 5-7 minutes until golden and crispy. Serve warm.

Scrumptious Chicken Panini

Serves: 1 | Total Time: 25 minutes

Ingredients

1 tablespoon mayonnaise

1 teaspoon yellow mustard

2 sandwich bread slices

1 deli chicken ham slice

1 provolone cheese slice

1 mozzarella slice

½ avocado, sliced

½ tomato, sliced

Salt and black pepper to taste

½ teaspoon sesame seeds

1 teaspoon butter, melted

Directions

Start by preheating your air fryer to 350°F. Rub mayonnaise and mustard on the inside of each bread slice. Top 1 bread slice with chicken ham, provolone and mozzarella cheese, avocado, sesame seeds, and tomato slices. Season with salt and pepper. Then, close the sandwiches with the other bread slice.

Brush the top and bottom of the sandwich lightly with melted butter. Place the sandwich in the frying basket and Bake for 6 minutes, flipping once. Serve.

Exotic Chicken Drumsticks

Serves: 1 | Total Time: 30 minutes

Ingredients

½ tablespoon lime juice

½ tablespoon oyster sauce

2 chicken drumsticks

¼ tablespoon peanut oil

½ tablespoon honey

½ tablespoon brown sugar

½ tablespoon ketchup

1 tablespoon pineapple juice

Directions

Preheat the air fryer to 350°F. Drizzle half of the lime juice and oyster sauce on the drumsticks. Transfer to the frying basket and drizzle with peanut oil. Shake the basket to coat. Bake for 18 minutes until the drumsticks are almost done.

Meanwhile, combine the remaining lime juice and oyster sauce along with the honey, sugar, ketchup, and pineapple juice in a small bowl. When the chicken is done, transfer to the bowl and coat the chicken with the sauce.

Put the bowl in the basket and cook for 5-7 minutes, turning halfway, until golden and cooked through. Serve and enjoy your exotic chicken drumsticks!

Mustard Chicken Tenders

Serves: 1 | Total Time: 20 minutes

Ingredients

¼ teaspoon dried oregano

¼ teaspoon granulated garlic

¼ teaspoon granulated onion

½ teaspoon chili powder

¼ teaspoon sweet paprika

Salt and black pepper to taste

1 chicken breast, sliced

½ tablespoon yellow mustard

Directions

Start by preheating your air fryer to 375°F. Mix together oregano, salt, garlic, onion, chili powder, paprika, and black pepper in a small bowl. Coat the chicken with mustard in a bowl. Sprinkle the seasoning mix over the chicken.

Place the chicken in the greased frying basket and Air Fry for 7-8, flipping once until cooked through. Serve immediately.

Barbecue Chicken Thighs

Serves: 1 | Total Time: 30 minutes

Ingredients

2 boneless, skinless chicken thighs

1 teaspoon barbecue sauce

1 small garlic clove, minced

¼ teaspoon lemon zest

1 teaspoon fresh parsley, chopped

½ tablespoon lemon juice

Directions

Coat the chicken with barbecue sauce, garlic, and lemon juice in a medium bowl. Leave to marinate for 10 minutes.

Preheat your air fryer to 380°F. When ready to cook, remove the chicken from the bowl and shake off any drips. Arrange the chicken thighs in the air fryer and Bake for 16-18 minutes, until golden and cooked through. Serve topped with lemon zest and parsley. Enjoy!

Air Fried Chicken with Black Beans

Serves: 1 | Total Time: 30 minutes

Ingredients

1 chicken breast, cubed

1 green onion, chopped

½ cup mixed bell pepper strips

½ jalapeño pepper, minced

1 teaspoon olive oil

¼ cup canned black beans

2 tablespoons salsa

1 teaspoon Mexican chili powder

Directions

Start by preheating your air fryer to 400°F. Combine the chicken, green onion, bell pepper, jalapeño, and olive oil in a bowl. Transfer to a bowl to the frying basket and Air Fry for 10 minutes, stirring once during cooking. When done, stir in the black beans, salsa, and chili powder. Air Fry for 7-10 minutes or until cooked through. Serve warm.

Texas-Style Chicken Breast

Serves: 1 | Total Time: 20 minutes

Ingredients

¼ teaspoon crushed red pepper flakes

½ red pepper, deseeded and diced

Salt to taste

1 chicken breast

¼ teaspoon garlic powder

¼ teaspoon onion powder

¼ teaspoon ground cumin

¼ teaspoon ancho chile powder

¼ teaspoon sweet paprika

¼ teaspoon oregano

½ tomato, chopped

¼ diced red onion

1 ½ tablespoon fresh lime juice

½ avocado, diced

½ tablespoon chopped cilantro

Directions

Preheat the air fryer to 380°F. Stir together salt, garlic and onion powder, cumin, ancho chili powder, paprika, Mexican oregano, and pepper flakes in a bowl. Spray the chicken with cooking oil and rub with the spice mix.

Air Fry the chicken for 10 minutes, flipping once until browned and fully cooked. Repeat for both pieces of chicken. Mix the onion and lime juice in a bowl. Fold in the avocado, cilantro, red pepper, salt, and tomato, and coat gently. To serve, top the chicken with guacamole salsa.

French Chicken Cordon Bleu

Serves: 1 | Total Time: 25 minutes

Ingredients

1 deli ham slice, halved lengthwise
½ tablespoon grated Grana Padano cheese
1 chicken breast
Salt and black pepper to taste
2 Swiss cheese slices

1 small egg
2 tablespoons bread crumbs
¼ teaspoon garlic powder
¼ teaspoon onion powder
¼ teaspoon mustard powder

Directions

Preheat the air fryer to 400°F. Season the chicken with salt and pepper. On the chicken, put the slice of ham and cheese on the top. Roll the chicken tightly, then set aside. Beat the egg and egg white in a shallow bowl.

Put the crumbs, Grana padano cheese, garlic, onion, and mustard powder in a second bowl. Dip the cutlet in the egg bowl and then in the crumb mix. Press so that they stick to the chicken.

Put the roll of chicken seam side down in the greased frying basket and Air Fry for 12-14 minutes, flipping once until golden and cooked through. Serve.

Juicy Chicken Thighs

Serves: 1 | Total Time: 35 minutes

Ingredients

2 boneless, skinless chicken thighs
¼ tablespoon Italian seasoning
Salt and black pepper to taste
1 garlic clove, minced

¼ teaspoon apple cider vinegar
½ teaspoon honey
¼ tablespoon Dijon mustard

Directions

Preheat your air fryer to 400°F. Season the chicken with Italian seasoning, salt, and black pepper. Place in the greased frying basket and Bake for 15 minutes, flipping once halfway through cooking.

While the chicken is cooking, add garlic, honey, vinegar, and Dijon mustard in a saucepan and stir-fry over medium heat for 4 minutes or until the sauce has thickened and warmed through. Transfer the thighs to a serving dish and drizzle with honey-mustard sauce. Serve and enjoy!

Sticky Chicken Drumsticks

Serves: 1 | Total Time: 45 minutes

Ingredients

2 chicken drumsticks

¼ tablespoon chicken seasoning

¼ teaspoon dried chili flakes

Salt and black pepper to taste

1 tablespoon honey

¼ cup barbecue sauce

Directions

Start by preheating your air fryer to 390°F. Season drumsticks with chicken seasoning, chili flakes, salt, and pepper. Place one batch of drumsticks in the greased frying basket and Air Fry for 18-20 minutes, flipping once until golden.

While the chicken is cooking, combine honey and barbecue sauce in a small bowl. Remove the drumsticks to a serving dish. Drizzle honey-barbecue sauce over and serve.

Sweet & Sour Chicken with Rice

Serves: 1 | Total Time: 25 minutes

Ingredients

¼ (8-oz) can pineapple chunks, drained, 1 tablespoon juice reserved

½ cup cooked long-grain rice

1 chicken breast, cubed

¼ red onion, chopped

½ tablespoon peanut oil

½ peeled peach, cubed

¼ tablespoon cornstarch

¼ teaspoon ground ginger

¼ teaspoon chicken seasoning

Directions

Start by preheating your air fryer to 400°F. Combine the chicken, red onion, pineapple, and peanut oil in a metal bowl, then put the bowl in the fryer. Air Fry for 8-10 minutes, remove, and stir. Toss the peach in and put the bowl back into the fryer for 3 minutes. Slide out and stir again.

Mix the reserved pineapple juice, corn starch, ginger, and chicken seasoning in a bowl, then pour over the chicken mixture and stir well. Put the bowl back into the fryer and cook for 3 more minutes or until the chicken is cooked through and the sauce is thick. Serve over cooked rice.

Curry-Yogurt Chicken

Serves: 1 | Total Time: 35 minutes + marinating time

Ingredients

2 teaspoons plain yogurt

½ tablespoon lemon juice

¼ teaspoon curry powder

¼ teaspoon ground cinnamon

1 garlic clove, minced

¼-inch piece ginger, grated

1 teaspoon olive oil

1 chicken breast

Directions

Mix the yogurt, lemon juice, curry powder, cinnamon, garlic, ginger, and olive oil in a bowl. Slice the chicken, without cutting, all the way through by making thin slits, then toss it into the yogurt mix. Coat well and let marinate for 10 minutes.

Preheat your air fryer to 360°F. Take the chicken out of the marinade, letting the extra liquid drip off. Toss the rest of the marinade away. Air Fry the chicken for 10 minutes. Turn each piece, then cook for 8-13 minutes more until cooked through and no pink meat remains. Serve.

Kale & Ricotta-Stuffed Chicken

Serves: 1 | Total Time: 30 minutes

Ingredients

1 tablespoon ricotta cheese

½ cup Tuscan kale, chopped

1 chicken breast

¼ tablespoon chicken seasoning

Salt and black pepper to taste

¼ teaspoon paprika

Directions

Start by preheating your air fryer to 370°F. Soften the ricotta cheese in a microwave-safe bowl for 15 seconds. Combine in a bowl along with Tuscan kale. Set aside.

Cut 4-5 slits in the top of each chicken breast about ¾ of the way down. Season with chicken seasoning, salt, and pepper. Place the chicken with the slits facing up in the greased frying basket. Lightly spray the chicken with oil. Bake for 6-8 minutes. Slide-out and stuff the cream cheese mixture into the chicken slits. Sprinkle ½ teaspoon of paprika and cook for another 3 minutes. Serve and enjoy!

Awesome Cajun Chicken Kebabs

Serves: 1 | Total Time: 30 minutes

Ingredients

½ teaspoon lemon juice

1 teaspoon olive oil

½ tablespoon chopped parsley

¼ teaspoon dried oregano

¼ Cajun seasoning

1 chicken breast, cubed

4 cherry tomatoes

½ zucchini, cubed

Directions

Start by preheating your air fryer to 400°F. Combine the lemon juice, olive oil, parsley, oregano, and Cajun seasoning in a bowl. Toss in the chicken and stir, making sure all pieces are coated. Allow marinating for 10 minutes.

Take 2 bamboo skewers and poke the chicken, tomatoes, and zucchini, alternating the pieces. Use a brush to put more marinade on them, then lay them in the air fryer. Air Fry the kebabs for 15 minutes, turning once, or until the chicken is cooked through, with no pink showing. Get rid of the leftover marinade. Serve and enjoy!

Roasted Hawaiian Chicken

Serves: 1 | Total Time: 25 minutes

Ingredients

½ (15-oz) can diced pineapple

½ kiwi, sliced

1 tablespoon coconut aminos

½ teaspoon honey

1 garlic clove, minced

Salt and black pepper to taste

¼ teaspoon paprika

1 chicken breast

Directions

Start by preheating your air fryer to 360°F. Stir together pineapple, kiwi, coconut aminos, honey, garlic, salt, paprika, and pepper in a small bowl. Place the chicken in a baking dish that fits in the fryer. Spread half of the pineapple mixture over the top of the chicken.

Transfer the dish into the frying basket. Roast for 8 minutes, then flip the chicken. Spread the rest of the pineapple mixture over the top of the chicken and Roast for another 8-10 until the chicken is done. Allow sitting for 5 minutes. Serve and enjoy!

Buffalo Sauce Chicken Drumettes

Serves: 1 | Total Time: 30 minutes

Ingredients

2 chicken drumettes

¼ teaspoon garlic powder

¼ tablespoon chicken seasoning

Black pepper to taste

1 tablespoon Buffalo wings sauce

1 spring onion, sliced

Directions

Preheat your air fryer to 400°F. Sprinkle garlic, chicken seasoning, and pepper on the drumettes. Place them in the fryer and spray with cooking oil. Air Fry for 10 minutes, shaking the basket once.

Transfer the drumettes to a large bowl. Drizzle with Buffalo wing sauce and toss to coat. Place in the fryer and Fry for 7-8 minutes, until crispy. Allow to cool slightly. Top with spring onions. Serve.

Tikka Masala Chicken Thighs

Serves: 1 | Total Time: 35 minutes + marinating time

Ingredients

2 boneless, skinless chicken thighs

1 tablespoon yogurt

1 garlic clove, minced

¼ tablespoon lime juice

¼ teaspoon ginger-garlic paste

¼ teaspoon garam masala

¼ teaspoon ground turmeric

¼ teaspoon red pepper flakes

Salt to taste

1 vine tomato, quartered

½ tablespoon chopped cilantro

1 lime wedge

Directions

Mix yogurt, garlic, lime juice, ginger paste, garam masala, turmeric, flakes, and salt in a bowl.

Place the thighs in a zipper bag and pour in the marinade. Massage the chicken to coat and refrigerate for 2 hours.

Preheat your air fryer to 400°F. Remove the chicken from the bag and discard the marinade. Put the chicken in the greased frying basket and Arr Fry for 13-15 minutes, flipping once until browned and thoroughly cooked. Set chicken aside and cover with foil. Spray tomatoes with cooking oil.

Place in the frying basket and Bake for 8 minutes, shaking the basket once until soft and slightly charred. Sprinkle with salt. Top the chicken and veggies with cilantro and lemon wedges.

Summer Chicken Salad

Serves: 1 | Total Time: 25 minutes

Ingredients

1 chicken breast, cubed
½ small red onion, sliced
¼ red bell pepper, sliced
¼ cup green beans, sliced

1 teaspoon ranch salad dressing
½ tablespoon lemon juice
¼ teaspoon dried basil
4 oz spring mix

Directions

Start by preheating your air fryer to 400°F. Put the chicken, red onion, red bell pepper, and green beans in the frying basket and Roast for 10-13 minutes until the chicken is cooked through. Shake the basket at least once while cooking.

As the chicken is cooking, combine the ranch dressing, lemon juice, and basil. When the cooking is done, remove the chicken and veggies to a bowl and let cool slightly. Pour the dressing over. Stir to coat. Serve with spring mix.

Mom's Chicken Wings

Serves: 1 | Total Time: 35 minutes

Ingredients

4 chicken wings, split at the joint
¼ tablespoon water
¼ tablespoon sesame oil
½ tablespoon Dijon mustard

¼ teaspoon chili powder
¼ tablespoon tamari
¼ teaspoon honey
¼ teaspoon white wine vinegar

Directions

Start by preheating your air fryer to 400°F. Coat the wings with sesame oil. Place them in the frying basket and Air Fry for 16-18 minutes, tossing once or twice.

Whisk the remaining ingredients in a bowl. Reserve. When ready, transfer the wings to a serving bowl. Pour the previously prepared sauce over and toss to coat. Serve immediately.

Delicious Sweet Chicken Biryani

Serves: 1 | Total Time: 30 minutes

Ingredients

1 chicken breast, cubed
1 teaspoon olive oil
1 tablespoon cornstarch
¼ teaspoon curry powder

¼ apple, chopped
1 tablespoon chicken broth
1 tablespoon dried cranberries
¼ cooked basmati rice

Directions

Start by preheating your air fryer to 380°F. Combine the chicken and olive oil, then add some corn starch and curry powder. Mix to coat, then add the apple and pour the mix into a baking pan.

Put the pan in the air fryer and Bake for 8 minutes, stirring once. Add the chicken broth, cranberries, and ½ tablespoon of water and continue baking for 10 minutes, letting the sauce thicken. The chicken should be lightly charred and cooked through. Serve warm with basmati rice.

Dark Bacon-Wrapped Chicken Breast

Serves: 1 | Total Time: 35 minutes

Ingredients

1 tablespoon mayonnaise
1 tablespoon sour cream
1 teaspoon ketchup
½ teaspoon yellow mustard

¼ teaspoon dark brown sugar
¼ pound chicken tenders
¼ teaspoon dried parsley
1 bacon slice

Directions

Preheat the air fryer to 370°F. Combine the mayonnaise, sour cream, ketchup, mustard, and brown sugar in a bowl and mix well, then set aside. Sprinkle the chicken with the parsley and wrap it in a slice of bacon.

Put the wrapped chicken in the frying basket in a single layer and Air Fry for 18-20 minutes, flipping once until the bacon is crisp. Serve with sauce.

Tender Saharan-Style Chicken Strips

Serves: 1 | Total Time: 30 minutes

Ingredients

1 chicken breast, cut into strips
1 teaspoon olive oil
½ tablespoon cornstarch
1 garlic clove, minced
¼ cup chicken broth

1 teaspoon lemon juice
½ teaspoon honey
¼ teaspoon ras el hanout
½ cup cooked couscous

Directions

Start by preheating your air fryer to 400°F. Mix the chicken and olive oil in a bowl, then add the cornstarch. Stir to coat. Add the garlic and transfer to a baking pan. Put the pan in the fryer. Bake for 10 minutes. Stir at least once during cooking.

When done, pour in the broth, lemon juice, honey, and ras el hanout. Bake for 6-9 minutes or until the sauce is thick and the chicken cooked through with no pink showing. Serve with couscous.

Prosciutto Chicken Rolls

Serves: 1 | Total Time: 30 minutes

Ingredients

¼ cup chopped broccoli
1 tablespoon grated cheddar cheese
1 scallion, sliced
1 garlic clove, minced
2 prosciutto thin slices
2 tablespoons cream cheese

Salt and black pepper to taste
¼ teaspoon dried oregano
¼ teaspoon dried basil
1 chicken breast
1 tablespoon chopped cilantro

Directions

Start by preheating your air fryer to 375°F. Combine broccoli, scallion, garlic, cheddar cheese, cream cheese, salt, pepper, oregano, and basil in a small bowl. Prepare the chicken by placing it between two pieces of plastic wrap. Pound the chicken with a meat mallet or heavy can until it is evenly ½-inch thickness. Slice the chicken in two pieces.

Top each with a slice of prosciutto and spoon ½ of the cheese mixture in the center of each chicken piece. Fold each one over the filling and transfer to a greased baking dish.

Place the dish in the frying basket and bake for 8 minutes. Flip the chicken and bake for another 8-12 minutes. Allow resting for 5 minutes. Serve warm sprinkled with cilantro and enjoy!

Thyme & Rosemary Chicken Breast

Serves: 1 | Total Time: 25 minutes + marinating time

Ingredients

1 chicken breast
1 teaspoon rosemary, minced
1 teaspoon thyme, minced

Salt and black pepper to taste
1 teaspoon chopped cilantro
½ teaspoon lime juice

Directions

Place chicken in a resealable bag. Add rosemary, thyme, salt, pepper, cilantro, and lime juice. Seal the bag and toss to coat, then place in the refrigerator for 2 hours.

Preheat your air fryer to 400°F. Place the chicken in the greased frying basket. Spray it with cooking oil. Air Fry for 6-7 minutes, then flip the chicken. Cook for another 3 minutes. Serve and enjoy!

Strawberry-Glazed Chicken Tenders

Serves: 1 | Total Time: 20 minutes + marinating time

Ingredients

¼ pound chicken tenderloins

1 teaspoon strawberry preserves

1 teaspoon chopped basil

½ teaspoon orange juice

¼ teaspoon orange zest

Salt and black pepper to taste

Directions

Combine all ingredients, except for basil, in a bowl. Marinade in the fridge covered for 30 minutes.

Preheat your air fryer to 350°F. Place the chicken tenders in the frying basket and Air Fry for 4-6 minutes. Shake the basket gently and turn over the chicken. Cook for 5 more minutes. Top with basil.

Popcorn Chicken with Baby Potatoes

Serves: 1 | Total Time: 30 minutes

Ingredients

½ tablespoon cooked popcorn, ground

Salt and black pepper to taste

2 chicken tenders

1 tablespoon bread crumbs

¼ teaspoon dried thyme

¼ tablespoon olive oil

½ carrot, sliced

2 baby potatoes

Directions

Start by preheating your air fryer to 380°F. Season the chicken tenders with salt and pepper. In a shallow bowl, mix the crumbs, popcorn, thyme, and olive oil until combined. Coat the chicken with the mixture. Press firmly so the crumbs adhere.

Arrange the carrot slices and baby potatoes in the greased frying basket and top them with the chicken tenders. Bake for 9-10 minutes. Shake the basket and continue cooking for another 9-10 minutes until the vegetables are tender. Serve and enjoy!

Italian Chicken Piccata Linguine

Serves: 1 | Total Time: 30 minutes

Ingredients

1 chicken breast, cut into cutlets

Salt and black pepper to taste

1 small egg

¼ cup bread crumbs

¼ teaspoon Italian seasoning

¼ tablespoon butter

¼ cup chicken broth

¼ teaspoon onion powder

1 tablespoon fino sherry

¼ lemon, juiced and zested

¼ tablespoon capers

2 lemon slices

1 cup cooked linguine

Directions

Start by preheating your air fryer to 370°F. Place the breast between two sheets of parchment paper. Using a rolling pin, pound the chicken to a ¼-inch thickness and season with salt and pepper. Beat the eggs with 1 teaspoon of the caper liquid in a bowl.

Put the bread crumbs, Parmesan cheese, onion powder, and Italian seasoning in a second bowl and stir. Dip the cutlet in the egg mixture and then in the crumb mix. Put the cutlet in the greased frying basket. Air Fry for 6 minutes, flipping once until crispy and golden.

Melt butter in a skillet over medium heat. Stir in broth, sherry, lemon juice, zest, and pepper. Bring to a boil and cook for 3-4 minutes until the sauce is reduced by half. Remove. Stir in capers. Top with chicken. Pour the sauce over and garnish with lemon slices. Serve warm.

Easy Creole Drumettes

Serves 4 | Total Time: 50 minutes

Ingredients

2 chicken drumettes
¼ cup flour
¼ cup heavy cream
¼ cup sour cream

¼ cup bread crumbs
¼ teaspoon Creole seasoning
1 teaspoon melted butter

Directions

Start by preheating your air fryer to 370°F. Combine chicken drumettes and flour in a bowl. Shake away excess flour and set aside. Mix the heavy cream and sour cream in a bowl. In another bowl, combine bread crumbs and Creole seasoning.

Dip floured drumettes in cream mixture, then dredge them in crumbs. Place the chicken drumettes in the greased frying basket and Air Fry for 20 minutes, tossing once and brushing with melted butter. Let rest for a few minutes on a plate and serve.

Red Grapes Chicken Salad

Serves: 1 | Total Time: 30 minutes

Ingredients

6 halved seedless red grapes
1 chicken breast, cubed
Salt and black pepper to taste
1 tablespoon mayonnaise

½ teaspoon lemon juice
1 teaspoon chopped parsley
¼ cup chopped celery
¼ shallot, diced

Directions

Start by preheating your air fryer to 350°F. Sprinkle chicken with salt and pepper. Place the chicken cubes in the frying basket and Air Fry for 9 minutes, flipping once. In a salad bowl, combine the cooked chicken, mayonnaise, lemon juice, parsley, grapes, celery, and shallot and let chill covered in the fridge for 1 hour up to overnight.

Curry Chicken Nuggets

Serves: 1 | Total Time: 30 minutes

Ingredients

1 boneless, skinless chicken breast

1 teaspoon curry powder

Salt and black pepper to taste

1 small egg, beaten

1 teaspoon sesame oil

¼ cup panko bread crumbs

¼ cup coconut yogurt

1 teaspoon mango chutney

1 teaspoon mayonnaise

Directions

Preheat the air fryer to 400°F. Cube the chicken into 1-inch pieces and sprinkle with curry powder, salt, and pepper; toss to coat.

Beat together the egg and sesame oil in a shallow bowl and scatter the panko onto a separate plate. Dip the chicken in the egg, then in the panko, and press to coat. Lay the coated nuggets on a wire rack as you work.

Set the nuggets in the greased frying basket and Air Fry for 7-10 minutes, shaking once halfway through cooking. While the nuggets are cooking, combine the yogurt, chutney, and mayonnaise in a small bowl. Serve the nuggets with the dipping sauce.

Lemony Chicken Bulgogi

Serves: 1 | Total Time: 30 minutes + marinating time

Ingredients

2 boneless, skinless chicken thighs, cubed

½ cucumber, thinly sliced

1 tablespoon apple cider vinegar

1 garlic clove, minced

¼ teaspoon ground ginger

¼ teaspoon red pepper flakes

½ teaspoon honey

Salt to taste

½ teaspoon tamari

1 teaspoon sesame oil

½ teaspoon honey

2 tablespoons lemon juice

¼ teaspoon lemon zest

2 scallions, chopped

½ cup cooked white rice

½ teaspoon roasted sesame seeds

Directions

In a bowl, toss the cucumber, vinegar, half of the garlic, half of the ginger, pepper flakes, honey, and salt and store in the fridge covered. Combine the tamari, sesame oil, granular honey, lemon juice, remaining garlic, remaining ginger, and chicken in a large bowl. Toss to coat and marinate in the fridge for 10 minutes.

Preheat your air fryer to 350°F. Place chicken in the frying basket, do not discard excess marinade. Air Fry for 10-12 minutes, shaking once and pouring excess marinade over. Place the chicken bulgogi over the cooked rice and scatter with scallion greens, pickled cucumbers, and sesame seeds. Serve and enjoy!

Spanish-Style Chicken Skewers

Serves: 1 | Total Time: 35 minutes

Ingredients

5 ounces yellow summer squash, sliced
1 chicken breast
1 tablespoon plain yogurt
1 teaspoon olive oil
¼ teaspoon sweet pimentón
¼ teaspoon dried thyme

Sea salt to taste
¼ teaspoon garlic powder
¼ teaspoon ground cumin
½ red bell pepper
4 large green olives

Directions

Preheat the air fryer to 400°F. Combine yogurt, olive oil, pimentón, thyme, cumin, salt, and garlic in a bowl and add the chicken. Stir to coat. Cut the bell peppers into 1-inch pieces. Remove the chicken from the marinade; set aside the rest of the marinade.

Thread the chicken, peppers, squash, and olives onto 2 skewers. Brush the skewers with marinade. Discard any remaining marinade. Lay the kebabs in the frying basket. Add a raised rack and put the rest of the kebabs on it. Bake for 18-23 minutes, flipping once around minute 10. Serve hot.

Chinese-Style Chicken Thighs

Serves: 1 | Total Time: 35 minutes

Ingredients

2 boneless, skinless chicken thighs
½ tablespoon tamari sauce
½ tablespoon lemon juice
¼ teaspoon ground ginger
Black pepper to taste

1 tablespoon cornstarch
1 tablespoon chicken stock
½ tablespoon hoisin sauce
½ teaspoon light brown sugar
½ teaspoon sesame seeds

Directions

Preheat the air fryer to 400°F. After cubing the chicken thighs, put them in a cake pan. Add tamari sauce, lemon juice, ginger, and black pepper. Mix and let marinate for 10 minutes. Remove the chicken and coat it in cornstarch; set aside.

Add the stock, hoisin sauce, brown sugar to the cake pan and mix well. Put the pan in the frying basket and Air Fry for 5-8 minutes or until bubbling and thick, stirring once.

Remove and set aside. Put the chicken in the frying basket and Fry for 15-18 minutes, shaking the basket once. Remove the chicken to the sauce in the pan and return to the fryer to reheat for 2 minutes. Sprinkle with the sesame seeds and serve.

Air Fryed Citrus Chicken

Serves: 1 | Total Time: 25 minutes

Ingredients

1 chicken breast, cubed

Salt and black pepper to taste

1 tablespoon cornstarch

¼ cup orange juice

1 tablespoon orange marmalade

1 tablespoon ketchup

¼ teaspoon ground ginger

½ tablespoon soy sauce

¼ cup edamame beans

Directions

Preheat the air fryer to 375°F. Sprinkle the chicken with salt and pepper. Coat with cornstarch and set aside on a wire rack. Mix the orange juice, marmalade, ketchup, ginger, soy sauce, and the remaining cornstarch in a cake pan, then stir in the beans.

Set the pan in the frying basket and Bake for 5-8 minutes, stirring once during cooking, until the sauce is thick and bubbling. Remove from the fryer and set aside.

Put the chicken in the frying basket and fry for 10-12 minutes, shaking the basket once. Stir the chicken into the sauce and beans in the pan. Return to the fryer and reheat for 2 minutes.

Strawberry & Hazelnut Chicken Salad

Serves 1 | Total Time: 30 minutes

Ingredients

¼ chicken breast, cubed

Salt and pepper to taste

1 tsp mayonnaise

¼ tbsp lime juice

1 cup lettuce, torn

1 tsp chopped hazelnuts

1 tsp chopped celery

3 diced strawberries

Directions

Preheat your air fryer to 350°F. Sprinkle chicken with salt and pepper. Place it in the frying basket. Air Fry for 9 minutes, shaking once. Remove and leave it to cool. Whisk the mayonnaise and lime juice in a bowl. Drizzle the lettuce and top wih chicken, hazelnuts, celery, and strawberries. Serve.

French-Syle Seasoned Chicken Breast

Serves: 1 | Total Time: 30 minutes

Ingredients

1 tablespoon tomato sauce

½ teaspoon yellow mustard

½ teaspoon apple cider vinegar

½ teaspoon honey

1 garlic clove, minced

½ Fresno pepper, minced

¼ teaspoon onion powder

1 chicken breast

Directions

Preheat your air fryer to 370°F. Mix tomato sauce, mustard, apple cider vinegar, honey, garlic, Fresno pepper, and onion powder in a bowl. Use a brush to rub the mix over the chicken breast.

Put the chicken in the air fryer and Grill for 10 minutes. Remove it, turn it, and rub with more sauce. Cook further for about 5 minutes. Remove the basket and flip the chicken. Add more sauce, return to the fryer, and cook for 3-5 more minutes or until the chicken is cooked through.

Honey-Glazed Chicken Thighs

Serves: 1 | Total Time: 25 minutes

Ingredients

2 boneless, skinless chicken thighs
1 teaspoon balsamic vinegar
½ teaspoon honey
½ teaspoon brown sugar
¼ teaspoon whole-grain mustard

1 tablespoon soy sauce
1 garlic clove, minced
Salt and black pepper to taste
¼ teaspoon smoked paprika
¼ chopped shallots

Directions

Start by preheating your air fryer to 375°F. Whisk vinegar, honey, sugar, soy sauce, mustard, garlic, salt, pepper, and paprika in a small bowl. Arrange the chicken in the frying basket and brush the top of each with some of the vinegar mixture. Air Fry for 7 minutes, then flip the chicken.

Brush the tops with the rest of the vinegar mixture and Air Fry for another 5 to 8 minutes. Allow resting for 5 minutes before slicing. Serve warm sprinkled with shallots.

Herby & Breaded Chicken Thighs

Serves: 1 | Total Time: 55 minutes + marinating time

Ingredients

2 chicken thighs
½ cup flour
¼ teaspoon dried basil
¼ teaspoon dried thyme
¼ teaspoon dried shallot powder

¼ teaspoon smoked paprika
¼ teaspoon mustard powder
¼ teaspoon celery salt
¼ cup kefir
½ teaspoon honey

Directions

Preheat the air fryer to 370°F. Combine the flour, salt, basil, thyme, shallot, paprika, mustard powder, and celery salt in a bowl. Pour into a glass jar. Mix the kefir and honey in a large bowl and add the chicken; stir to coat. Marinate for 15 minutes at room temperature.

Remove the chicken from the kefir mixture; discard the rest. Put the flour mix onto a plate and dip the chicken. Shake gently and put on a wire rack for 10 minutes. Line the frying basket with round parchment paper with holes punched in it. Place the chicken and spray with cooking oil. Air Fry for 18-25 minutes, flipping once. Serve hot.

TURKEY RECIPES

Turkey Steak with Green Salad

Serves: 1 | Total Time: 20 minutes

Ingredients

1 tablespoon shaved Parmesan cheese

½ teaspoon grated Parmesan cheese

1 (5 ounces) turkey breast steak

Salt and black pepper to taste

1 small egg, beaten

2 tablespoons bread crumbs

¼ teaspoon dried thyme

½ cup baby spinach

½ cup ounces watercress

½ teaspoon olive oil

½ teaspoon lemon juice

1 spring onion, chopped

1 lemon wedge

Directions

Place the steak between two sheets of parchment paper. Pound the turkey to ¼-inch thick cutlets using a meat mallet or rolling pin. Season with Salt and black pepper to taste.

Put the beaten egg in a shallow bowl. Put the crumbs, thyme, and Parmesan in a second shallow bowl. Dip the cutlet in the egg bowl and then in the crumb mix. Press the crumbs so that they stick to the turkey.

Preheat your air fryer to 400°F. Fry the turkey in the greased frying basket for 8 minutes, flipping once until golden and cooked through. Repeat for all cutlets. Put the spinach, spring onion, and watercress in a bowl. Toss with olive oil, lemon juice, salt, and pepper. Serve turkey on a plate topped with salad. Garnish with lemon wedge and shaved Parmesan cheese. Serve.

Goat Cheese Turkey Roulade

Serves: 1 | Total Time: 55 minutes

Ingredients

5 ounces boneless turkey breast, skinless

Salt and black pepper to taste

1 oz goat cheese

¼ tablespoon marjoram

¼ tablespoon sage

1 garlic clove, minced

1 teaspoon olive oil

1 teaspoon chopped cilantro

Directions

Start by preheating your air fryer to 380°F. Butterfly the turkey breast with a sharp knife and season with salt and pepper. Mix together the goat cheese, marjoram, sage, and garlic in a bowl. Spread the cheese mixture over the turkey breast, then roll it up tightly, tucking the ends underneath.

Put the turkey breast roulade onto a piece of aluminum foil, wrap it up, and place it into the air fryer. Bake for 30 minutes. Turn the turkey breast, brush the top with oil, and then continue to cook for another 10-15 minutes. Slice and serve sprinkled with cilantro.

Easy Turkey Tenderloin

Serves: 1 | Total Time: 45 minutes

Ingredients

5 ounces boneless, skinless turkey tenderloin
Salt and black pepper to taste
¼ teaspoon garlic powder
¼ teaspoon chili powder

¼ teaspoon dried thyme
¼ lemon, juiced
½ tablespoon chopped cilantro

Directions

Start by preheating your air fryer to 350°F. Dry the turkey completely with a paper towel, then season with salt, pepper, garlic powder, chili powder, and thyme. Place the turkey in the basket.

Squeeze the lemon juice over the turkey and bake for 10 minutes. Turn the turkey and bake for another 10 to 15 minutes. Allow resting for 10 minutes before slicing. Serve sprinkled with cilantro.

Simple Herby Turkey

Serves: 1 | Total Time: 35 minutes

Ingredients

1 (5 ounces) turkey tenderloin
½ tablespoon olive oil
Salt and black pepper to taste

¼ tablespoon minced rosemary
¼ tablespoon minced thyme
¼ tablespoon minced sage

Directions

Preheat the air fryer to 350°F. Brush the tenderloin with olive oil and sprinkle with salt and pepper. Mix rosemary, thyme, and sage, then rub the seasoning onto the meat. Put the tenderloins in the frying basket and Bake for 22-27 minutes, flipping once until cooked through. Lay the turkey on a serving plate, cover with foil, and let stand for 5 minutes. Slice before serving.

Turkey Tacos

Serves: 1 | Total Time: 15 minutes

Ingredients

½ cup cooked turkey breast, pulled
2 tortilla wraps
1 tablespoon grated Swiss cheese

¼ small red onion, sliced
½ tablespoon Mexican chili sauce

Directions

Start by preheating your air fryer to 400°F. Lay a tortilla wrap on a clean workspace, then spoon Swiss cheese, turkey, Mexican chili sauce, and red onion. Top with the other tortilla.

Spritz the top with cooking spray. Air Fry the quesadilla for 5-8 minutes. The cheese should be melted and the outside crispy. Serve.

Berry-Glazed Turkey Breast

Serves: 1 | Total Time: 1 Hour 25 minutes

Ingredients

¼ pound bone-in, skin-on turkey breast

½ tablespoon olive oil

Salt and black pepper to taste

¼ cup raspberries

¼ cup chopped strawberries

½ tablespoon balsamic vinegar

½ tablespoon butter, melted

¼ tablespoon honey mustard

¼ teaspoon dried rosemary

Directions

Preheat the air fryer to 350°F. Lay the turkey breast skin-side up in the frying basket, brush with the oil, and sprinkle with salt and pepper. Bake for 55-65 minutes, flipping twice.

Meanwhile, mix the berries, vinegar, melted butter, rosemary and honey mustard in a blender and blend until smooth. Turn the turkey skin-side up inside the fryer and brush with half of the berry mix. Bake for 5 more minutes.

Put the remaining berry mix in a saucepan and simmer for 3-4 minutes while the turkey cooks. When the turkey is done, let it stand for 10 minutes, then carve. Serve with the remaining glaze.

Taco-Seasoned Ground Turkey

Serves 1 | Total Time: 35 minutes

Ingredients

5 ounces boneless, skinless turkey breast

½ cup mild chunky salsa

¼ teaspoon taco seasoning

1 lime wedge for serving

Directions

Start by preheating your air fryer to 350°F. Add turkey to a baking pan and rub with taco seasoning. Pour mild chunky salsa over. Place the pan in the frying basket.

Air Fry for 30 minutes until the turkey is golden brown. Serve with lime wedges. Enjoy!

Turkey Ratatouille

Serves 1 | Total Time: 30 minutes

Ingredients

5 ounces boneless, skinless turkey breast, cubed

1 teaspoon grated Parmesan cheese

¼ eggplant, cubed

¼ zucchini, cubed

¼ bell pepper, diced

¼ fennel bulb, sliced

1 tsp salt

¼ teaspoon Italian seasoning

1 teaspoon olive oil

1 diced tomato

¼ teaspoon pasta sauce

¼ teaspoon basil leaves

Directions

Preheat your air fryer to 400°F. Mix the turkey, eggplant, zucchini, bell pepper, fennel, salt, Italian seasoning, and oil in a bowl. Place the turkey mixture in the frying basket.

Air Fry for 7 minutes. Transfer it to a cake pan. Mix in tomato and pasta sauce. Air Fry for 8 minutes. Scatter with Parmesan and basil. Serve and enjoy!

Herby & Breaded Turkey Cutlets

Serves: 1 | Total Time: 15 minutes

Ingredients

1 tablespoon bread crumbs
¼ teaspoon paprika
Salt and black pepper to taste
¼ teaspoon dried sage
¼ teaspoon garlic powder

¼ teaspoon ground cumin
1 small egg
1 (5-ounce) turkey breast
1 teaspoon chopped chervil

Directions

Start by preheating your air fryer to 380°F. Mix the bread crumbs, paprika, salt, black pepper, sage, cumin, and garlic powder in a bowl. Beat the egg in another bowl until frothy.

Dip the turkey into the egg mixture, then coat it in the bread crumb mixture. Put the breaded turkey in the frying basket. Bake for 4 minutes. Turn over, then Bake for 4 more minutes. Decorate with chervil and serve.

Effortless Garlicky Turkey

Serves: 1 | Total Time: 65 minutes

Ingredients

½ tablespoon butter, melted
1 garlic clove, minced
¼ teaspoon dried oregano
¼ teaspoon dried thyme

¼ teaspoon dried rosemary
Salt and black pepper to taste
5 ounces turkey breast
1 teaspoon chopped cilantro

Directions

Start by preheating your air fryer to 350°F.

Combine butter, garlic, oregano, salt, and pepper in a small bowl. Place the turkey breast on a plate and coat the entire turkey with the butter mixture. Put the turkey in the frying basket and scatter with thyme and rosemary.

Bake for 20 minutes. Flip the turkey so that the breast side is up, then bake for another 20-30 minutes until it has an internal temperature of 165°F. Allow resting for 10 minutes before carving. Serve sprinkled with cilantro.

SNACKS & SIDE DISHES

Classic French Fries

Serves: 1 | Total Time: 25 minutes

Ingredients

1 russet potato
½ tablespoon olive oil

½ tablespoon herbs de Provence

Directions

Start by preheating your air fryer to 400°F. Slice the potatoes lengthwise into ½-inch thick strips. In a bowl, whisk the olive oil and herbs de Provence. Toss in the potatoes to coat. Arrange them in a single and Air Fry for 18-20 minutes, shaking once, until crispy. Serve warm.

Crispy Sweet Potato Fries

Serves: 1 | Total Time: 20 minutes

Ingredients

1 tablespoon olive oil
1 sweet potato, sliced

¼ teaspoon dried thyme
Salt to taste

Directions

Start by preheating your air fryer to 390°F. Spread the sweet potato slices in the greased basket and brush with olive oil. Air Fry for 6 minutes. Remove the basket, shake, and sprinkle with thyme and salt. Cook for 6 more minutes or until lightly browned. Serve warm and enjoy!

Eggplant Fries

Serves: 1 | Total Time: 20 minutes

Ingredients

½ eggplant, sliced
¼ tablespoon shoyu
¼ teaspoon garlic powder

¼ teaspoon onion powder
1 teaspoon olive oil
½ tablespoon fresh basil, chopped

Directions

Preheat your air fryer to 390°F. Place the eggplant slices in a bowl and sprinkle the shoyu, garlic, onion, and oil on top. Coat the eggplant evenly. Place the eggplant in a single layer in the greased frying basket and Air Fry for 5 minutes. Remove and put the eggplant in the bowl again.

Toss the eggplant slices to coat evenly with the remaining liquid and put back in the fryer. Roast for another 3 minutes. Remove the basket and flip the pieces over to ensure even cooking. Roast for another 5 minutes or until the eggplant is golden. Top with basil and serve.

Avocado Fries

Serves: 1 | Total Time: 20 minutes

Ingredients

1 egg

2 tablespoons milk

Salt and black pepper to taste

½ cup crushed chili corn chips

1 tablespoon Parmesan cheese

½ avocado, sliced into fries

Directions

Start by preheating your air fryer to 375°F. In a bowl, beat egg and milk. In another bowl, add crushed chips, Parmesan cheese, salt, and pepper. Dip avocado fries into the egg mixture, then dredge into the crushed chips mixture to coat.

Place avocado fries in the greased frying basket and Air Fry for 5 minutes. Serve immediately.

Easy Kale Chips

Serves: 1 | Total Time: 15 minutes

Ingredients

¼ cup Greek yogurt

½ tablespoon lemon juice

¼ teaspoon mustard powder

¼ teaspoon dried dill

½ tablespoon ground walnuts

½ bunch of curly kale

½ tablespoon olive oil

Salt and black pepper to taste

Directions

Start by preheating your air fryer to 390°F. Mix together yogurt, lemon juice, mustard powder, ground walnuts, and dill until well blended. Set aside. Cut off the stems and ribs from the kale, then cut the leaves into 3-inch pieces.

In a bowl, toss the kale with olive oil, salt, and pepper. Arrange the kale in the fryer and Air Fry for 2-3 minutes. Shake the basket, then cook for another 2-3 minutes or until the kale is crisp. Serve the chips with Greek sauce.

Effortless Carrot Chips

Serves: 1 | Total Time: 15 minutes

Ingredients

2 small carrots, cut into coins

½ tablespoon sesame oil

Salt and black pepper to taste

Directions

Start by preheating your air fryer to 375°F. Combine all ingredients in a bowl. Place carrots in the frying basket and Roast for 10 minutes, tossing once. Serve right away.

Golden Beet Fries with Yogurt

Serves: 1 | Total Time: 40 minutes

Ingredients

1 peeled golden beet

¼ cup plain Greek yogurt

½ tablespoon fresh dill, chopped

1 tablespoon lime juice

Salt to taste

1 small egg, beaten

½ cup panko bread crumbs

¼ teaspoon paprika

Directions

Start by preheating your air fryer to 375°F. Mix the yogurt, lime juice, and salt in a bowl, then pour the dip into a serving bowl. Sprinkle with dill, cover, and refrigerate. Slice the beets into 3-inch long sticks that are ½ inch thick.

Beat the eggs in a shallow bowl and combine the panko and paprika on a plate. Dip the fries in the egg, then the panko mixture, coating well. Put the beets in the frying basket and spray with cooking oil. Air Fry for 18-23 minutes or until crispy and golden. Serve with yogurt dip.

Breaded Okra Fries

Serves: 1 | Total Time: 25 minutes

Ingredients

¼ pound trimmed okra, cut lengthways

¼ teaspoon chili powder

1 teaspoon buttermilk

1 tablespoon chickpea flour

1 tablespoon cornmeal

Salt and black pepper to taste

Directions

Start by preheating your air fryer to 380°F. Set out 2 bowls. In one, add buttermilk. In the second, mix flour, cornmeal, chili powder, salt, and pepper. Dip the okra in buttermilk, then dredge in flour and cornmeal.

Transfer to the frying basket and spray the okra with oil. Air Fry for 10 minutes, shaking once halfway through cooking until crispy. Let cool for a few minutes and serve warm.

Homemade BBQ Potato Chips

Serves: 1 | Total Time: 30 minutes

Ingredients

1 scrubbed russet potato, sliced

½ teaspoon smoked paprika

¼ teaspoon chili powder

¼ teaspoon garlic powder

¼ teaspoon onion powder

¼ tablespoon smoked paprika

¼ teaspoon light brown sugar

Salt and black pepper to taste

2 teaspoons olive oil

Directions

Start by preheating your air fryer to 400°F. Combine all seasoning in a bowl. Set aside. In another bowl, mix potato chips, olive oil, black pepper, and salt until coated.

Place potato chips in the frying basket and Air Fry for 17 minutes, shaking 3 times. Transfer it to a bowl. Sprinkle with the bbq mixture and let sit for 15 minutes. Serve immediately.

Cheesy Zucchini Fries

Serves: 1 | Total Time: 35 minutes

Ingredients

½ pound thin zucchini chips

1 small egg

¼ cup bread crumbs

¼ cup grated Pecorino cheese

Salt and black pepper to taste

¼ cup mayonnaise

¼ tablespoon olive oil

¼ lemon, juiced

½ teaspoon garlic powder

Salt and black pepper to taste

Directions

Start by preheating your air fryer to 350°F. Beat eggs in a small bowl, then set aside. In another small bowl, stir together bread crumbs, Pecorino, salt, and pepper. Dip zucchini slices into the egg mixture, then in the crumb mixture.

Place them in the greased frying basket and Air Fry for 10 minutes. Remove and set aside to cool. Mix the mayonnaise, olive oil, lemon juice, garlic, salt, and pepper in a bowl to make aioli. Serve aioli with chips and enjoy.

Old-Fashioned Onion Rings

Serves: 1 | Total Time: 30 minutes

Ingredients

1 sweet yellow onion

½ cup buttermilk

¾ cup flour

1 tablespoon cornstarch

Salt and black pepper to taste

¾ teaspoon garlic powder

½ teaspoon dried oregano

1 cup bread crumbs

Directions

Start by preheating your air fryer to 390°F. Cut the onion into ½-inch slices. Separate the onion slices into rings. Place the buttermilk in a bowl and set aside.

In another bowl, combine the flour, cornstarch, salt, pepper, and garlic. Stir well and set aside. In a separate bowl, combine the breadcrumbs with oregano and salt. Dip the rings into the buttermilk, dredge in flour, dip into the buttermilk again, and then coat into the crumb mixture.

Put in the greased frying basket without overlapping. Spritz them with cooking oil and Air Fry for 13-16 minutes, shaking once or twice until the rings are crunchy and browned. Serve hot.

Cajun-Style Fried Pickles

Serves: 1 | Total Time: 20 minutes

Ingredients

4 oz canned pickle slices

2 tablespoons flour

½ tablespoon cornmeal

¼ teaspoon Cajun seasoning

¼ tablespoon dried parsley

1 small egg, beaten

¼ teaspoon hot sauce

¼ cup buttermilk

½ tablespoon light mayonnaise

½ tablespoon chopped chives

¼ teaspoon garlic powder

¼ teaspoon onion powder

Salt and black pepper to taste

Directions

Start by preheating your air fryer to 350°F. Mix flour, cornmeal, Cajun seasoning, and parsley in a bowl. Put the beaten egg in a small bowl nearby. One at a time, dip a pickle slice in the egg, then roll in the crumb mixture. Gently press the crumbs so they stick to the pickle.

Place the chips in the greased frying basket and Air Fry for 7-9 minutes, flipping once until golden and crispy. In a bowl, whisk hot sauce, buttermilk, mayonnaise, chives, garlic and onion powder, salt, and pepper. Serve with pickles.

Almond Zucchini Fries

Serves: 1 | Total Time: 30 minutes

Ingredients

¼ cup grated Pecorino cheese

1 zucchini, cut into fries

Salt to taste

1 small egg

½ tablespoon almond milk

¼ cup almond flour

Directions

Start by preheating your air fryer to 370°F. Distribute zucchini fries evenly over a paper towel, sprinkle with salt, and let sit for 10 minutes to pull out moisture. Pat them dry with paper towels. In a bowl, beat egg and almond milk.

In another bowl, combine almond flour and Pecorino cheese. Dip fries in egg mixture and then dredge them in flour mixture. Place zucchini fries in the lightly greased frying basket and Air Fry for 10 minutes, flipping once. Serve.

Crispy Turnip Chips

Serves: 1 | Total Time: 20 minutes

Ingredients

1 tablespoon olive oil

1 peeled, thinly sliced turnip

Salt to taste

½ cup hummus

Directions

Start by preheating your air fryer to 325°F. Put the sliced turnip in the greased frying basket, spread the pieces out, and drizzle with olive oil. Air Fry for 10-12 minutes, shaking the basket twice. Sprinkle with salt and serve with hummus.

Vegetable Fritters with Green Dip

Serves: 1 | Total Time: 40 minutes

Ingredients

½ grated carrot

½ medium zucchini

½ minced small onion

1 garlic clove, minced

1 small egg

1 tablespoon flour

1 tablespoon bread crumbs

Salt and black pepper to taste

¼ teaspoon ground cumin

½ avocado, peeled and pitted

1 tablespoon plain Greek yogurt

¼ teaspoon lime juice

¼ tablespoon white vinegar

½ tablespoon chopped cilantro

Directions

Start by preheating your air fryer to 380°F. Place the carrot, zucchini, onion, garlic, egg, flour, bread crumbs, salt, pepper, and cumin in a large bowl. Mix until well combined.

Scoop out equal portions of the vegetable mixture and form them into patties. Arrange the patties on the greased basket. Air Fry them for about 5-6 minutes, flip over, and continue cooking for another 5-6 minutes or until the fritters are golden and crisp.

While the fritters are cooking, prepare the avocado dip. Mash the avocado in a small bowl to the desired texture. Stir in yogurt, white vinegar, chopped cilantro, lime juice, and salt. When the fritters are done, transfer to a serving plate along with the avocado dip. Serve warm.

Ranch Potato Chips

Serves: 1 | Total Time: 30 minutes

Ingredients

¼ teaspoon dry ranch seasoning

Salt and black pepper to taste

1 sliced fingerling potato

1 teaspoon olive oil

1 tablespoon white wine vinegar

Directions

Preheat your air fryer to 400°F. In a bowl, combine ranch mix, salt, and pepper. Reserve ½ teaspoon for garnish. In another bowl, mix sliced fingerling potato with the vinegar and stir around. Let soak in the vinegar water for at least thirty minutes, then drain the potato chips and pat them dry.

Place potato chips and spread with olive oil until coated. Sprinkle with the ranch mixture and toss to coat. Place potato chips in the frying basket and Air Fry for 16 minutes, shaking 2 times. Transfer it to a bowl. Sprinkle with the reserved mixture and let sit for 15 minutes. Serve.

Mexican-Style Red Potato Fries

Serves: 1 | Total Time: 35 minutes

Ingredients

¼ teaspoon smoked paprika

¼ tablespoon lemon juice

1 purple red potato

½ teaspoon olive oil

¼ teaspoon minced thyme

¼ teaspoon cayenne pepper

Sea salt to taste

¼ cup Greek yogurt

½ chipotle chile, minced

½ tablespoon adobo sauce

Directions

Start by preheating your air fryer to 400°F. Cut the potato lengthwise into thin strips and put them in a bowl. Spray olive oil all over them and toss until the strips are evenly coated. Add the potatoes to the frying basket and Air Fry for 10-14 minutes. Shake them up at around minute 5.

Mix the yogurt, chipotle chiles, adobo sauce, paprika, and lemon juice in a bowl, then put it in the refrigerator. When cooking is finished, put the potatoes on a large plate and toss thyme, cayenne pepper, and sea salt on top. Serve with this Mexican dip. Enjoy!

Air Fried Veggies

Serves: 1 | Total Time: 55 minutes

Ingredients

2 red potatoes, cut into rounds

½ onion, diced

½ green bell pepper, diced

½ red bell pepper, diced

1 tablespoon olive oil

Salt and black pepper to taste

½ teaspoon garlic powder

½ teaspoon harissa seasoning

Directions

Combine all ingredients in a large bowl and mix until potatoes are well coated and seasoned.

Preheat your air fryer to 350°F. Pour all of the contents in the bowl into the frying basket. Bake for 35 minutes, shaking every 10 minutes, until golden brown and soft. Serve hot.

Spicy Parsnip Chips

Serves: 1 | Total Time: 35 minutes

Ingredients

¼ teaspoon smoked paprika

¼ teaspoon chili powder

¼ teaspoon garlic powder

¼ teaspoon onion powder

¼ teaspoon cayenne pepper

¼ teaspoon granulated sugar

Salt to taste

1 parsnip, cut into chips

1 teaspoon olive oil

Directions

Start by preheating your air fryer to 400°F. Mix all spices in a bowl and reserve. In another bowl, combine parsnip chips, olive oil, and salt. Place parsnip chips in the lightly greased frying basket.

Air Fry for 12 minutes, shaking once. Transfer the chips to a bowl, toss in seasoning mix, and let sit for 15 minutes before serving.

Mediterranean Zucchini Fritters

Serves: 1 | Total Time: 35 minutes

Ingredients

2 tablespoons crumbled feta cheese
1 grated zucchini
1 tablespoon Parmesan cheese
1 minced green onion
¼ teaspoon garlic powder
½ tablespoon flour
½ tablespoon cornmeal

1 tablespoon butter, melted
1 small egg
1 teaspoon chopped fresh dill
1 teaspoon chopped fresh parsley
Salt and black pepper to taste
½ cup bread crumbs

Directions

Start by preheating your air fryer to 360°F. Place the grated zucchini into a clean kitchen towel and squeeze out as much liquid as possible. In a bowl, combine all ingredients except for the breadcrumbs.

Shape 12 equal-sized patties out of the mixture. Coat the fritters with breadcrumbs and arrange them on a baking pan. Place it in the frying basket and Air Fry for 10-12 minutes, flipping once.

American Jackfruit Fritters

Serves: 1 | Total Time: 30 minutes

Ingredients

¼ (20-oz) can jackfruit, chopped
1 small egg, beaten
¼ tablespoon Dijon mustard
¼ tablespoon mayonnaise
¼ tablespoon prepared horseradish
½ tablespoon grated yellow onion
½ tablespoon chopped parsley

½ tablespoon chopped nori
½ tablespoon flour
¼ tablespoon Cajun seasoning
¼ teaspoon garlic powder
Salt to taste
2 lemon wedges

Directions

In a bowl, combine jackfruit, egg, mustard, mayonnaise, horseradish, onion, parsley, nori, flour, Cajun seasoning, garlic, and salt. Let chill in the fridge for 15 minutes.

Preheat your air fryer to 350°F. Divide the mixture into 12 balls. Place them in the frying basket and Air Fry for 10 minutes. Serve with lemon wedges.

Air Fried Spinach

Serves: 1 | Total Time: 20 minutes

Ingredients

5 oz spinach

1 tablespoon lemon juice

1 tablespoon olive oil

Salt and black pepper to taste

¼ teaspoon garlic powder

¼ teaspoon onion powder

Directions

Start by preheating your air fryer to 350°F. Place the spinach in a bowl, drizzle with lemon juice and olive oil, and massage with your hands. Scatter with salt, pepper, garlic, and onion and gently toss to coat well. Arrange the leaves in a single layer and Bake for 3 minutes. Shake and Bake for another 1-3 minutes until brown. Let cool completely.

Beer-Battered Onion Rings

Serves: 1 | Total Time: 25 minutes

Ingredients

1 sliced onion, rings separated

½ cup flour

Salt and black pepper to taste

½ teaspoon garlic powder

½ cup beer

Directions

Start by preheating your air fryer to 350°F. In a mixing bowl, combine the flour, garlic powder, beer, salt, and black pepper. Dip the onion rings into the bowl and lay the coated rings in the basket.

Air Fry for 15 minutes, shaking the basket several times during cooking to jostle the onion rings and ensure a good, even fry. Once ready, the onions should be crispy and golden brown. Serve.

Breaded Pickle Chips

Serves: 1 | Total Time: 25 minutes

Ingredients

1 dill pickle, sliced

½ cup breadcrumbs

1 small egg, beaten

A pinch of white pepper

½ teaspoon curry powder

¼ teaspoon mustard powder

Directions

Start by preheating your air fryer to 350°F. Combine the breadcrumbs, curry, mustard powder, and white pepper in a mixing bowl. Coat the pickle slices with the crumb mixture; then dip into the eggs, then dip again into the dry ingredients.

Arrange the coated pickle pieces on the greased frying basket in an even layer. Air Fry for 15 minutes, shaking the basket several times during cooking until crisp. Serve warm.

Garlicky Kale Chips

Serves: 1 | Total Time: 20 minutes

Ingredients

¼ tablespoon chili powder

¼ teaspoon garlic powder

1 cup kale, torn

1 teaspoon olive oil

Sea salt to taste

Directions

Start by preheating your air fryer to 390°F. Coat the kale with olive oil, chili, and garlic powder. Put it in the frying basket and Air Fry until crispy, about 5-6 minutes, shaking the basket at around 3 minutes. Toss some sea salt on the kale chips once they are finished and serve.

Ricotta-Stuffed Jalapeños

Serves: 1 | Total Time: 15 minutes

Ingredients

4 jalapeño peppers

2 oz ricotta cheese

2 tablespoons grated cheddar cheese

1 tablespoon bread crumbs

Directions

Start by preheating your air fryer to 340°F. Cut jalapeños in half lengthwise. Clean out the seeds and membrane. Set aside. Microwave ricotta cheese in a small bowl for 15 seconds to soften.

Stir in cheddar cheese to combine. Stuff each jalapeño half with the cheese mixture. Top the poppers with bread crumbs. Place in the air fryer and lightly spray with cooking oil. Bake for 5-6 minutes. Serve warm.

Mustard Green Chips with Curry Sauce

Serves: 1 | Total Time: 20 minutes

Ingredients

½ cup plain yogurt

½ tablespoon lemon juice

¼ tablespoon curry powder

¼ bunch of mustard greens

1 teaspoon olive oil

Sea salt to taste

Directions

Start by preheating your air fryer to 390°F. Using a sharp knife, remove and discard the ribs from the mustard greens. Slice the leaves into 2-3-inch pieces. Transfer them to a large bowl, then pour in olive oil and toss to coat.

Air Fry for 5-6 minutes. Shake at least once. The chips should be crispy when finished. Sprinkle with a little bit of sea salt. Mix the yogurt, lemon juice, salt, and curry in a small bowl. Serve the greens with the sauce. Enjoy!

Southern Spicy Okra Chips

Serves: 1 | Total Time: 20 minutes

Ingredients

1 egg

¼ cup whole milk

2 tablespoons bread crumbs

2 tablespoons cornmeal

¼ tablespoon Cajun seasoning

Salt and black pepper to taste

¼ teaspoon chili pepper

¼ pound okra, sliced

½ tablespoon butter, melted

Directions

Start by preheating your air fryer to 400°F. Beat the egg and milk in a bowl. In another bowl, combine the remaining ingredients, except okra and butter. Dip okra chips in the egg mixture, then dredge them in the breadcrumbs mixture.

Place okra chips in the greased frying basket and Roast for 7 minutes, shake once and brush with melted butter. Serve right away.

Sweet-Glazed Carrots

Serves: 1 | Total Time: 25 minutes

Ingredients

2 carrots, cut into spears

1 tablespoon orange juice

2 teaspoons balsamic vinegar

1 teaspoon avocado oil

1 teaspoon clear honey

½ teaspoon dried rosemary

Salt to taste

¼ teaspoon lemon zest

Directions

Start by preheating your air fryer to 390°F. Put the carrots in a baking pan. Add the orange juice, balsamic vinegar, oil, honey, rosemary, salt, and zest. Stir well.

Roast for 15-18 minutes, shaking them once or twice until the carrots are bright orange, glazed, and tender. Serve while hot.

Mexican Pimiento Strips

Serves: 1 | Total Time: 35 minutes

Ingredients

¼ (4-ounce) jar chopped pimientos, including juice

2 oz shredded sharp cheddar cheese

1 tablespoon mayonnaise

½ tablespoon cream cheese

Salt and black pepper to taste

1 teaspoon chopped parsley

2 sandwich bread slices

1 tablespoon butter, melted

Directions

In a bowl, mix the cheddar cheese, cream cheese, pimientos, mayonnaise, salt, parsley and pepper. Let chill covered in the fridge for 30 minutes.

Preheat your air fryer to 350°F. Spread pimiento mixture over one bread slice, then top with the other slice and press down just enough to not smoosh cheese out of the sandwich edges. Brush the top and bottom of each sandwich lightly with melted butter.

Place the sandwich in the frying basket and Grill for 6 minutes, flipping once. Slice each sandwich into 16 sections and serve warm.

Asian-Style Brussels Sprouts

Serves: 1 | Total Time: 20 minutes

Ingredients

½ pound Brussels sprouts

½ tablespoon maple syrup

½ teaspoon white miso

1 teaspoon toasted sesame oil

½ teaspoon soy sauce

1 garlic clove, minced

½ teaspoon grated fresh ginger

¼ teaspoon Gochugaru chili flakes

Directions

Start by preheating your air fryer to 390°F. Place the Brussels sprouts in the greased basket, spray with oil and Air Fry for 10-14 minutes, tossing once until crispy, tender, and golden. In a bowl, combine maple syrup and miso. Whisk until smooth.

Add the sesame oil, soy sauce, garlic, ginger, and Gochugaru flakes. Stir well. When the Brussels sprouts are done, add them to the bowl and toss with the sauce. Serve immediately.

Easy Breaded Mushrooms

Serves: 1 | Total Time: 30 minutes

Ingredients

¼ cup panko bread crumbs

½ cup white mushrooms

¼ cup flour

1 small egg, beaten

¼ teaspoon smoked paprika

1 garlic clove, minced

Salt and black pepper to taste

¼ cup arrabbiata sauce

Directions

Preheat the air fryer to 400°F. Put the flour on a plate. Mix the egg, garlic, and salt in a shallow bowl. Mix the panko bread crumbs, smoked paprika, salt, and pepper on a separate plate.

Cut the mushrooms through the stems into quarters. Dip the mushrooms in flour, then the egg, then in the panko mix. Press to coat, then put on a wire rack and set aside.

Add the mushrooms to the frying basket in a single layer and spray with cooking oil. Air Fry for 6-8 minutes, flipping them once until crisp. Serve warm with arrabbiata sauce for dipping.

Hot Cholula Avocado Fries

Serves: 1 | Total Time: 20 minutes

Ingredients

1 small egg, beaten
2 tablespoons flour
1 tablespoon almond flour

¼ teaspoon Cholula sauce
Salt to taste
1 peeled avocado half

Directions

Start by preheating your air fryer to 380°F. Mix the egg and Cholula sauce in a bowl. In another bowl, combine the remaining ingredients, except for the avocado.

Submerge avocado halves in the egg mixture and dredge them into the dry mix to coat. Place them in the lightly greased frying basket and Air Fry for 4-6 minutes. Serve immediately.

Quickly-Fried Beans with Greek Sauce

Serves: 1 | Total Time: 10 minutes

Ingredients

1 small egg
1 tablespoon flour
¼ teaspoon paprika
¼ teaspoon garlic powder
Salt to taste
2 teaspoons bread crumbs

¼ lemon zest
¼ pound whole string beans
¼ cup Greek yogurt
½ tablespoon lemon juice
¼ teaspoon cayenne pepper

Directions

Start by preheating your air fryer to 380°F. Whisk the egg and 2 tablespoons of water in a bowl until frothy. Sift the flour, paprika, garlic powder, and salt in another bowl, then stir in the crumbs.

Dip each string bean into the egg mixture, then roll into the bread crumb mixture. Put the string beans in a single layer in the greased frying basket.

Air Fry them for 5 minutes until the breading is golden brown. Stir the yogurt, lemon juice and zest, salt, and cayenne in a small bowl. Serve the bean fries with lemon-yogurt sauce.

Grandma's Potato Wedges

Serves: 1 | Total Time: 65 minutes

Ingredients

1 russet potato, cut into wedges
1 garlic head
1 tablespoon olive oil
2 tablespoons mayonnaise

½ tablespoon lemon juice
½ teaspoon Worcestershire sauce
¼ teaspoon cayenne pepper
Salt and black pepper to taste

½ teaspoon chili powder	1 tablespoon dried Italian herbs
¼ teaspoon ground cumin	2 tablespoons Parmesan cheese

Directions

Preheat your air fryer to 400°F. Cut off the garlic head top and drizzle with olive oil. Wrap loosely in foil and transfer to the frying basket. Cook for 30 minutes. Remove from the air fryer and open the foil.

Cook the garlic for 10 minutes, then squeeze the cloves out of their place in the head. Chop and transfer all but ½ teaspoon to a small bowl. Stir in mayonnaise, lemon juice, Worcestershire, and cayenne pepper. Cover and refrigerate.

Toss potatoes with the rest of the olive oil as well as salt, black pepper, Italian herbs, Parmesan cheese, chili powder, cumin, and the remaining chopped garlic. When coated, place the wedges in the frying basket in a single layer. Air Fry for 10 minutes, then shake the basket.

Air Fry for another 8-10 minutes until potatoes are tender. Bring out the garlic aioli. Place the potato wedges on a serving dish along with the aioli for dipping. Serve warm.

Easy Air-Fried Edamame

Serves: 1 | Total Time: 15 minutes

Ingredients

½ cup edamame, shelled and boiled	¼ teaspoon garlic powder
2 tablespoons flour	Salt to taste
2 tablespoons panko breadcrumbs	½ tablespoon olive oil

Directions

Preheat your air fryer to 375°F. Mix flour, panko crumbs, garlic powder, and salt in a bowl. In another bowl, coat the edamame with olive oil. Add the edamame to the flour mixture and toss to coat. Add them to the frying basket in one layer. Air Fry until golden brown on both sides and crisp around the edges, about 2 minutes per side. Serve warm with your favorite dipping sauce.

Breaded Herby Artichokes

Serves: 1 | Total Time: 25 minutes

Ingredients

4 canned artichoke hearts	¼ cup panko bread crumbs
1 egg	¼ teaspoon dried thyme
¼ cup all-purpose flour	¼ teaspoon dried parsley

Directions

Start by preheating your air fryer to 380°F. Set out three small bowls. In the first, add flour. In the second, beat the eggs. In the third, mix the crumbs, thyme, and parsley. Dip the artichoke in the flour, then dredge in the egg, then in the bread crumb. Place the breaded artichokes in the greased frying basket. Air Fry for 8 minutes, flipping them once until just browned and crisp. Serve.

FISH & SEAFOOD

Classic Fish & Chips

Serves: 1 | Total Time: 40 minutes

Ingredients

1 russet potato, peeled
1 tablespoon olive oil
2 tilapia fillets
¼ cup flour
Salt and black pepper to taste

½ teaspoon Old Bay seasoning
½ lemon, zested
1 egg, beaten
½ cup panko bread crumbs
2 tablespoons tartar sauce

Directions

Preheat the air fryer to 400°F. Slice the potatoes into ½-inch-thick chips and drizzle with olive oil. Sprinkle with salt. Add the fries to the frying basket and Air Fry for 12-16 minutes, shaking once. Remove the potatoes to a plate. Cover loosely with foil to keep warm.

Sprinkle the fish with salt and season with black pepper, lemon zest, and Old Bay seasoning, then lay on a plate. Put the egg in a shallow bowl and spread the panko on a separate plate. Dip the fish in the flour, then the egg, then the panko. Press to coat completely.

Add half the fish to the frying basket and spray with cooking oil. Set a raised rack on the frying basket, top with the other half of the fish, and spray with cooking oil. Air Fry for 8-10 minutes until the fish flakes. Serve the fish and chips with tartar sauce.

Cod Fingers with Broccoli Dip

Serves: 1 | Total Time: 40 minutes

Ingredients

1 cod fillet, cut into chunks
¼ cup broccoli florets
1 tablespoon grated Parmesan
1 garlic clove, peeled
½ tablespoon sour cream
½ tablespoon lemon juice

½ tablespoon olive oil
1 egg white
¼ cup panko bread crumbs
¼ teaspoon dried dill
Salt and black pepper to taste

Directions

Preheat the air fryer to 400°F. Put the broccoli and garlic in the greased frying basket and Air Fry for 5-7 minutes or until tender. Remove to a blender and add sour cream, lemon juice, olive oil, and ½ teaspoon of salt and process until smooth. Set the sauce aside.

Beat the egg whites until frothy in a shallow bowl. On a plate, combine the panko, Parmesan, dill, pepper, and the remaining ½ teaspoon of salt. Dip the cod fillets in the egg whites, then the breadcrumbs, pressing to coat.

Put half the cubes in the frying basket and spray with cooking oil. Air Fry for 6-8 minutes or until the fish is cooked through. Serve the fish with the sauce and enjoy!

Lemon Herb Salmon

Serves: 1 | Total Time: 30 minutes

Ingredients

1 salmon fillet

1 teaspoon olive oil

1 garlic clove, minced

¼ teaspoon lemon zest

¼ teaspoon lemon juice

1 tsp fresh dill, chopped

Salt and black pepper to taste

1 lemon wedge

Directions

Start by preheating your air fryer to 380°F. Coat the salmon fillet with olive oil, salt, and pepper to taste. In a small bowl, combine garlic, lemon zest, and lemon juice. Apply the mix over salmon.

Place the fish in the greased air fryer basket and Air Fry for 10-12 mins, checking for flakiness. Garnish topped with fresh dill and serve with lemon wedge. Enjoy!

Mediterranean Cod Croquettes

Serves: 1 | Total Time: 30 minutes + marinating time

Ingredients

¼ cup instant mashed potatoes

1 raw cod fillet, flaked

1 small egg, beaten

¼ cup sour cream

1 tablespoon olive oil

1 tablespoon chopped fresh thyme

½ shallot, minced

1 garlic clove, minced

¼ cup bread crumbs

½ teaspoon lemon juice

Salt and black pepper to taste

¼ teaspoon dried basil

1 tablespoon Greek yogurt

¼ teaspoon harissa paste

½ teaspoon chopped fresh dill

Directions

In a bowl, combine fish, 1/2 of the beaten egg, sour cream, instant mashed potatoes, olive oil, thyme, shallot, garlic, 1 tablespoon of the bread crumbs, salt, dill, lemon juice, and pepper; mix well. Refrigerate for 30 minutes. Mix yogurt, harissa paste, and basil in a bowl until blended. Set aside.

Preheat your air fryer to 350°F. Take the fish mixture out of the refrigerator. Knead and shape the mixture into 2 longs. In a bowl, place the remaining egg.

In a second bowl, add the remaining bread crumbs. Dip the croquettes into the egg and shake off the excess drips. Then, roll the logs into the breadcrumbs. Place the croquettes in the greased frying basket. Air Fry for 10 minutes, flipping once until golden. Serve with the yogurt sauce.

Chili Lime Sea Bass

Serves: 1 | Total Time: 25 minutes

Ingredients

1 sea bass fillet

1 tsp olive oil

¼ teaspoon chili powder

¼ teaspoon cumin

¼ teaspoon lime zest

¼ teaspoon lime juice

Salt and black pepper to taste

Fresh cilantro for garnish

Directions

Start by preheating your air fryer to 380°F. Brush with olive oil, season with chili powder, cumin, salt, and pepper. Sprinkle lime zest over the fish.

Transfer the fish to the greased basket and Air Fry for 10-12 minutes, flipping once. Squeeze lime juice over the cooked sea bass and garnish with fresh cilantro. Serve immediately and enjoy!

Fish Goujons with Tartar Sauce

Serves: 1 | Total Time: 20 minutes

Ingredients

1 tablespoon flour

Salt and black pepper to taste

¼ teaspoon smoked paprika

¼ teaspoon dried oregano

½ teaspoon dried thyme

1 small egg

1 haddock fillet

½ lemon, thinly sliced

1 tablespoon tartar sauce

Directions

Preheat your air fryer to 400°F. Combine flour, salt, pepper, paprika, thyme, and oregano in a wide bowl. Whisk egg and 1 teaspoon water in another wide bowl. Slice the fillet into 4 strips.

Dip the strips in the egg mixture. Then roll them in the flour mixture and coat completely. Arrange the fish strips on the greased frying basket. Air Fry for 4 minutes. Flip the fish and Air Fry for another 4 to 5 minutes until crisp. Serve warm with lemon slices and tartar sauce on the side.

Spanish Andalucian Calamari

Serves: 1 | Total Time: 25 minutes

Ingredients

¼ cup all-purpose flour

1 teaspoon hot chili powder

1 egg

½ tablespoon milk

½ cup bread crumbs

Salt and black pepper to taste

½ pound calamari rings

1 lime wedge

¼ cup aioli sauce

Directions

Start by preheating your air fryer to 400°F. In a shallow bowl, add flour and hot chili powder. In another bowl, mix the egg and milk. In a third bowl, mix the breadcrumbs, salt, and pepper. Dip calamari rings in flour mix first, then in the egg mix and shake off excess. Roll the calamari ring through crumb mixture.

Place calamari rings in the greased frying basket. Air Fry for 4 minutes, tossing once. Squeeze lime wedge over calamari. Serve with aioli sauce.

Parmesan Perch Fillets

Serves: 1 | Total Time: 15 minutes

Ingredients

1 tablespoon grated Parmesan

Salt to taste

¼ teaspoon paprika

½ tablespoon chopped fresh dill

¼ teaspoon dried thyme

¼ teaspoon Dijon mustard

1 tablespoon bread crumbs

1 ocean perch fillet

1 lemon wedge

1 tablespoon chopped cilantro

Directions

Start by preheating your air fryer to 400°F. Combine salt, paprika, pepper, dill, mustard, thyme, Parmesan, and bread crumbs in a wide bowl. Coat all sides of the fillet in the breading, then transfer to the greased frying basket.

Air Fry for 8 minutes until the outside is golden and the inside is cooked through. Garnish with lemon wedge and sprinkle with cilantro. Serve and enjoy!

Effortless Fish Fingers

Serves: 1 | Total Time: 30 minutes

Ingredients

1 cod fillet, cut into sticks

¼ cup flour

1 small egg

1 tablespoon cornmeal

Salt and black pepper to taste

¼ teaspoon smoked paprika

½ lemon

Directions

Start by preheating your air fryer to 350°F. In a bowl, add ½ cup of flour. In another bowl, beat the egg and in a third bowl, combine the remaining flour, cornmeal, salt, black pepper and paprika.

Roll the sticks in the flour and shake off excess flour. Then, dip them in the egg. Lastly, dredge them in the cornmeal mixture. Place fish fingers in the greased frying basket and Air Fry for 10 minutes, flipping once. Serve with squeezed lemon.

Fish Nuggets with Tartar Sauce

Serves: 1 | Total Time: 20 minutes

Ingredients

1 tablespoon mayonnaise

1 tablespoon yellow mustard

1 diced dill pickle

Salt and black pepper to taste

1 small egg, beaten

1 tablespoon cornstarch

2 tablespoons flour

1 cod fillet, cut into sticks

Directions

In a bowl, whisk mayonnaise, mustard, pickles, salt, and pepper to form tarter sauce; set aside. Preheat your air fryer to 350°F. Add the beaten egg to a bowl. In another bowl, combine cornstarch, flour, salt, and pepper. Dip fish nuggets in the egg and roll them in the flour mixture. Place fish nuggets in the greased frying basket and Air Fry for 10 minutes, flipping once. Serve with the sauce.

Easy & Spicy Shrimp

Serves: 1 | Total Time: 15 minutes

Ingredients

½ pound shelled tail-on shrimp, deveined

1 teaspoon grated Parmesan cheese

1 tablespoon butter, melted

¼ teaspoon cayenne pepper

¼ teaspoon garlic powder

¼ teaspoon Cajun seasoning

½ tablespoon lemon juice

Directions

Start by preheating your air fryer to 350°F. Toss the shrimp, melted butter, cayenne pepper, garlic powder and cajun seasoning in a bowl, place them in the greased frying basket.

Air Fry for 6 minutes, flipping once. Transfer it to a plate. Squeeze lemon juice over shrimp and stir in Parmesan cheese. Serve immediately.

Simple Air Fried Sardines

Serves: 1 | Total Time: 15 minutes

Ingredients

4 canned boneless, skinless sardines in mustard sauce

Salt and black pepper to taste

1 tablespoon bread crumbs

1 lemon wedge

1 teaspoon chopped parsley

Directions

Start by preheating your air fryer to 350°F. Add breadcrumbs, salt and pepper to a bowl. Roll sardines in the breadcrumbs to coat. Place them in the greased frying basket and Air Fry for 6 minutes, flipping once. Transfer them to a serving dish. Serve topped with parsley and lemon wedges.

Caribbean-Style Skewers

Serves: 1 | Total Time: 25 minutes

Ingredients

¼ can (4 oz) pineapple chunks, drained, liquid reserved

½ pound large shrimp, peeled and deveined

½ red bell pepper, chopped

1 scallions, chopped

½ tablespoon lemon juice

½ tablespoon olive oil

¼ teaspoon jerk seasoning

1 tablespoon cilantro, chopped

¼ teaspoon cayenne pepper

Directions

Preheat the air fryer to 370°F. Thread the shrimp, pineapple, bell pepper, and scallions onto 2 bamboo skewers. Mix pineapple juice with lemon juice, olive oil, jerk seasoning, and cayenne pepper. Brush every bit of the mix over the skewers.

Place the kebabs in the frying basket. Bake for 6-9 minutes and rearrange at about 4-5 minutes. Cook until the shrimp curl and pinken. Sprinkle with freshly chopped cilantro and serve.

Greek Prawn Cakes

Serves: 1 | Total Time: 25 minutes

Ingredients

¼ lb cooked prawns, minced

1 tablespoon Greek yogurt

¼ red onion, minced

½ celery stalk, minced

1 garlic clove, minced

¼ teaspoon dried basil

1 egg white

¼ cup breadcrumbs

Directions

Start by preheating your air fryer to 370°F. Combine the prawns, yogurt, red onion, celery, garlic, and basil in a bowl, then use your hands to make 2 ovals. Whisk the egg white in a shallow bowl and put the breadcrumbs on a plate. Dip each oval first in the egg white, then in the breadcrumbs. Air Fry the croquettes in the fryer for 7-10 minutes, turning them regularly. Serve hot.

Speedy & Scrumptious Air-Fried Scallops

Serves: 1 | Total Time: 20 minutes

Ingredients

¼ pound scallops

1 tablespoon olive oil

¼ teaspoon Old Bay seasoning

1 lemon wedge

Directions

Start by preheating your air fryer to 380°F. Toss scallops in olive oil and Old Bay seasoning. Air Fry: for 8-10 minutes, turning once or until golden. Squeeze fresh lemon over and serve.

MEAT RECIPES

Country-Style Pork Ribs

Serves: 1 | Total Time: 30 minutes

Ingredients

½ tablespoon cornstarch

1 tablespoon olive oil

¼ teaspoon mustard powder

¼ teaspoon thyme

¼ teaspoon garlic powder

¼ teaspoon paprika

Salt and black pepper to taste

4 country-style pork ribs

Directions

Start by preheating your air fryer to 400°F. Mix together cornstarch, olive oil, mustard powder, thyme, garlic powder, paprika, salt, and pepper in a bowl. Rub the seasoned mixture onto the ribs. Put the ribs into the frying basket. Bake for 14-16 minutes, flipping once until the ribs are crisp.

Sweet Pork Skewers

Serves: 1 | Total Time: 30 minutes

Ingredients

1 tablespoon apricot jam

½ tablespoon lemon juice

1 teaspoon olive oil

¼ teaspoon dried tarragon

1 pork tenderloin, cubed

2 pitted cherries, halved

1 pitted apricot, halved

Directions

Start by preheating your air fryer to 380°F. Toss the jam, lemon juice, olive oil, and tarragon in a big bowl and mix well. Place the pork in the bowl, then stir well to coat. Allow marinating for 10 minutes. Poke 2 metal skewers through the pork, cherries, and apricot, alternating ingredients.

Use a cooking brush to rub the marinade on the skewers, then place them in the air fryer. Toss the rest of the marinade. Air Fry the kebabs for 4-6 minutes on each side until the pork is cooked through and the fruit is soft. Serve!

Wasabi Pork Medallions

Serves: 1 | Total Time: 20 minutes + marinate time

Ingredients

2 pork medallions

¼ cup soy sauce

¼ tablespoon mirin

1 teaspoon olive oil

1 garlic clove, crushed

¼ teaspoon fresh grated ginger

¼ teaspoon wasabi paste

¼ tablespoon brown sugar

Directions

Place all ingredients, except for the pork, in a resealable bag and shake to combine. Add the pork medallions to the bag, shake again, and place in the fridge to marinate for 2 hours.

Preheat your air fryer to 360°F. Remove pork medallions from the marinade and place them in the frying basket in rows. Air Fry for 14-16 minutes or until the medallions are cooked through and juicy. Serve.

Sesame-Crusted Short Ribs

Serves: 1 | Total Time: 15 minutes + marinating time

Ingredients

1 teaspoon sesame seeds

4 pork short ribs

¼ cup soy sauce

1 teaspoon rice wine vinegar

¼ cup chopped onion

1 garlic clove, minced

1 tablespoon sesame oil

½ teaspoon sriracha sauce

1 tablespoon scallions, thinly sliced

Salt and black pepper to taste

Directions

Put short ribs in a resealable bag. Add the sesame seeds, soy sauce, rice wine vinegar, onion, garlic, sesame oil, sriracha sauce, half of the scallions, salt, and pepper. Seal the bag and toss to coat. Refrigerate for one hour.

Preheat your air fryer to 380°F. Place the short ribs in the air fryer. Bake for 8-10 minutes, flipping once until crisp. When the ribs are done, garnish with remaining scallions.

Herby Short Ribs

Serves: 1 | Total Time: 30 minutes

Ingredients

¼ teaspoon Worcestershire sauce

1 tablespoon olive oil

1 tablespoon balsamic vinegar

1 teaspoon chopped basil leaves

1 teaspoon chopped oregano

½ tablespoon honey

1 teaspoon chopped fresh sage

1 garlic clove, quartered

Salt to taste

5 ounces beef short ribs

Directions

Add all ingredients, except for the short ribs, to a plastic resealable bag and shake to combine. Reserve 2 tablespoons of balsamic mixture in a small bowl.

Place short ribs in the plastic bag and massage them. Seal the bag and let marinate in the fridge for 30 minutes up to overnight.

Preheat your air fryer to 325°F. Place short ribs in the frying basket and Bake for 16 minutes, turning them once and brushing with extra sauce. Serve warm.

Loaded Pork Strips with Rice

Serves: 1 | Total Time: 30 minutes + marinating time

Ingredients

1 tablespoon olive oil

¼ tablespoon tamari

¼ teaspoon red chili paste

1 teaspoon yellow mustard

¼ teaspoon granulated sugar

4 ounces pork shoulder strips

½ cup white rice, cooked

2 scallions, chopped

¼ teaspoon garlic powder

½ tablespoon lemon juice

¼ teaspoon lemon zest

Salt to taste

Directions

Add olive oil, tamari, chili paste, mustard, and sugar to a bowl and whisk well. Set aside half of the marinade. Toss pork strips in the remaining marinade and put in the fridge for 30 minutes.

Preheat your air fryer to 350°F. Place the pork strips in the frying basket and Air Fry for 16-18 minutes, tossing once. Transfer the cooked pork to the bowl along with the remaining marinade and toss to coat. Set aside.

In a medium bowl, stir in the cooked rice, garlic, lemon juice, lemon zest, and salt and cover. Spread on a serving plate. Arrange the pork strips over and top with scallions. Serve.

Texas-Style Pork Ribs

Serves 1 | Total Time: 45 minutes + marinating time

Ingredients

4 country-style pork ribs

¼ teaspoon garlic powder

¼ teaspoon onion powder

Salt and black pepper to taste

½ teaspoon lemon pepper

¼ teaspoon smoked paprika

¼ teaspoon cayenne pepper

¼ cup BBQ sauce

Directions

Combine garlic powder, onion powder, salt, pepper, lemon pepper, smoked paprika, and cayenne in a bowl. Add the ribs and toss to coat. Refrigerate for at least 1 hour.

Preheat your air fryer to 390°F. Brush the ribs with some BBQ sauce. Air Fry for 30-35 minutes, flipping and brushing them with the remaining BBQ sauce every 10 minutes.

Teriyaki Pork Ribs

Serves: 1 | Total Time: 30 minutes

Ingredients

4 pork ribs

1 teaspoon Teriyaki sauce

½ tablespoon honey

1 teaspoon ketchup

Black pepper to taste
¼ teaspoon ginger powder

¼ tablespoon sesame seeds

Directions

Start by preheating your air fryer to 380°F. Toss the ribs with all the ingredients, except for the sesame seeds, in a baking pan that fit in the fryer to coat. Air Fry for 16-18 minutes, flipping every 10 minutes. Top with sesame seeds and serve.

Fusion Flank Steak

Serves: 4 Total Time: 25 Minutes + marinating time

Ingredients

1 teaspoon cilantro, chopped
1 teaspoon chives, chopped
¼ teaspoon red pepper flakes
¼ jalapeño pepper, minced
1 teaspoon lime juice
½ teaspoon olive oil
Salt and black pepper to taste

½ teaspoon sesame oil
1 tablespoon tamari sauce
½ teaspoon honey
¼ tablespoon grated fresh ginger
1 green onion, minced
1 garlic clove, minced
1 (5 ounces) flank steak

Directions

Combine the jalapeño pepper, cilantro, chives, lime juice, olive oil, salt, and pepper in a bowl. Set aside. Mix the sesame oil, tamari sauce, honey, ginger, green onions, garlic, and pepper flakes in another bowl. Stir until the honey is dissolved. Put the steak into the bowl and massage the marinade onto the meat. Marinate for 2 hours in the fridge.

Preheat your air fryer to 390 F. Remove the steak from the marinade and place it in the greased frying basket. Air Fry for about 6 minutes, flip, and continue cooking for 6-8 more minutes. Allow to rest for a few minutes, slice thinly against the grain and top with the prepared dressing. Enjoy!

Classic Sirloin Finger Strips

Serves: 1 | Total Time: 25 minutes

Ingredients

5 ounces top sirloin strips
½ cup breadcrumbs
¼ teaspoon garlic powder
¼ teaspoon steak seasoning

1 egg, beaten
Salt and black pepper to taste
¼ tablespoon dried thyme

Directions

Start by preheating your air fryer to 350°F. Put the breadcrumbs, garlic powder, steak seasoning, thyme, salt, and pepper in a bowl and stir to combine. Add in the sirloin steak strips and toss to coat all sides. Dip into the beaten eggs, then dip again into the dry ingredients. Lay the coated steak pieces on the greased frying basket in an even layer. Air Fry for 16-18 minutes, turning once.

Stress-Free Beef Patties

Serves: 1 | Total Time: 30 minutes

Ingredients

¼ ounce ground beef
½ tablespoon ketchup
¼ tablespoon tamari

¼ teaspoon jalapeño powder
¼ teaspoon mustard powder
Salt and black pepper to taste

Directions

Start by preheating your air fryer to 350°F. Add the beef, ketchup, tamari, jalapeño, mustard salt, and pepper to a bowl and mix until evenly combined. Shape into 2 patties, then place them on the greased frying basket. Air Fry for 18-20 minutes, turning once. Serve and enjoy!

Authentic Beef Fajitas

Serves: 1 | Total Time: 15 minutes

Ingredients

4 oz sliced mushrooms
¼ onion, cut into half-moons
1 teaspoon olive oil
Salt and black pepper to taste

1 (5 ounces) strip steak
¼ teaspoon smoked paprika
¼ teaspoon fajita seasoning
1 teaspoon corn

Directions

Start by preheating your air fryer to 400°F. Combine the olive oil, onion, and salt in a bowl. Add the mushrooms and toss to coat. Spread in the frying basket. Sprinkle steak with salt, paprika, fajita seasoning and black pepper. Place steak on top of the mushroom mixture.

Air Fry for 9 minutes, flipping steak once. Let rest on a cutting board for 5 minutes before cutting in half. Serve the steak topped with mushrooms, corn, and onions and enjoy!

Air Fried Filet Mignon

Serves: 1 | Total Time: 30 minutes

Ingredients

1 filet mignon steak
¼ teaspoon garlic powder

Salt and black pepper to taste
1 teaspoon butter, melted

Directions

Start by preheating your air fryer to 370°F. Sprinkle the steaks with salt, garlic and pepper on both sides. Place them in the greased frying basket and Air Fry for 12 minutes to yield a medium-rare steak, turning twice. Transfer steaks to a cutting board, brush them with butter and let rest 5 minutes before serving.

Montreal-Style Rib Eye Steak

Serves: 1 | Total Time: 15 minutes

Ingredients

½ teaspoon Montreal steak seasoning

1 (5-oz) ribeye steak

½ tablespoon butter, melted

1 teaspoon chopped parsley

½ teaspoon fresh rosemary

Directions

Start by preheating your air fryer to 400°F. Sprinkle ribeye with steak seasoning and rosemary on both sides. Place it in the basket and Bake for 10 minutes, turning once. Remove it to a cutting board and drizzle with butter. Let rest for 5 minutes and scatter with parsley. Serve immediately.

Herby & Lemony Strip Steak

Serves: 1 | Total Time: 15 minutes

Ingredients

1 garlic clove, minced

¼ tablespoon lemon juice

1 teaspoon olive oil

Salt and black pepper to taste

1 teaspoon chopped parsley

¼ teaspoon chopped rosemary

¼ teaspoon chopped sage

1 (5 ounces) strip steak

Directions

In a small bowl, whisk all ingredients. Brush mixture over strip steak and let marinate covered in the fridge for 30 minutes.

Preheat your air fryer to 400°F. Place strip steak in the greased frying basket and Bake for 8 minutes until rare, turning once. Let rest on a cutting board for 5 minutes before serving.

Balsamic Veggie & Beef Skewers

Serves: 1 | Total Time: 25 minutes

Ingredients

1 teaspoon balsamic vinegar

1 teaspoon olive oil

¼ teaspoon dried oregano

Salt and black pepper to taste

1 (5 ounces) round steak, cubed

¼ red bell pepper, sliced

¼ yellow bell pepper, sliced

¼ cup cherry tomatoes

Directions

Preheat your air fryer to 390°F. Put balsamic vinegar, olive oil, oregano, salt, and pepper in a bowl and stir. Toss the steak in and allow to marinate for 10 minutes. Poke 2 metal skewers through the beef, bell peppers, and cherry tomatoes, alternating ingredients as you go. Place the skewers in the air fryer and Air Fry for 5-7 minutes, turning once. Serve and enjoy!

Party Cheeseburgers

Serves: 1 | Total Time: 20 minutes

Ingredients

¼ ounce ground beef

¼ teaspoon Worcestershire sauce

¼ teaspoon allspice

Salt and black pepper to taste

1 cheddar cheese slice

1 bun

Directions

Start by preheating your air fryer to 360°F. Combine beef, Worcestershire sauce, allspice, salt, and pepper in a large bowl. Shape the mixture into a patty. Place the burger in the greased frying basket and Air Fry for 8 minutes. Flip and cook for another 3-4 minutes. Top the burger with cheddar cheese and cook for another minute until the cheese melts. Transfer to a bun and serve.

European-Style Short Ribs

Serves: 1 | Total Time: 30 minutes

Ingredients

1/8 teaspoon Worcestershire sauce

1 teaspoon olive oil

1 tablespoon balsamic vinegar

1 tablespoon chopped basil leaves

1 tablespoon chopped oregano

1 teaspoon honey

1 tablespoon chopped fresh sage

1 garlic clove, slices

Salt to taste

2 beef short ribs

Directions

Add all ingredients, except for the short ribs, to a plastic resealable bag and shake to combine. Reserve 1 tablespoon of balsamic mixture in a small bowl. Place short ribs in the plastic bag and shake. Seal the bag and let marinate in the fridge for 30 minutes up to overnight.

Preheat your air fryer to 325°F. Place short ribs in the frying basket and Bake for 16 minutes, turning them once and brushing with extra sauce. Serve warm.

Classic Italian Beef Meatballs

Serves: 1 | Total Time: 35 minutes

Ingredients

1 teaspoon grated Parmesan

5 ounces ground beef

1 small egg, beaten

½ tablespoon tomato paste

¼ teaspoon Italian seasonings

1 tablespoon ricotta cheese

1 garlic clove, minced

1 tablespoon grated yellow onion

Salt and black pepper to taste

1 teaspoon almond flour

1 teaspoon chopped basil

½ cup marinara sauce

Directions

Start by preheating your air fryer to 400°F. In a large bowl, combine ground beef, egg, tomato paste, Italian seasoning, ricotta cheese, Parmesan cheese, garlic, onion, salt, pepper, flour, and basil. Form mixture into 2 meatballs. Add them to the greased frying basket and Air Fry for 20 minutes.

Warm the marinara sauce in a skillet over medium heat for 3 minutes. Add in cooked meatballs and roll them around in sauce for 2 minutes. Serve with sauce over the top.

Rosemary T-Bone Steak

Serves: 1 | Total Time: 20 minutes + chilling time

Ingredients

½ tablespoon butter, softened

¼ teaspoon lemon juice

1 garlic clove, minced

1 teaspoon minced fresh rosemary

1 (5 ounces) beef T-bone steak

Salt and black pepper to taste

¼ teaspoon onion powder

Directions

In a small bowl, whisk butter, lemon juice, onion powder, garlic, and rosemary. Transfer the butter mixture onto parchment paper. Roll into a log and spin ends to tighten. Let chill in the fridge for 2 hours. Remove the steak from the fridge 30 minutes before cooking. Season.

Preheat your air fryer to 400°F. Add the steak to the greased frying basket and Air Fry for 10 minutes, flipping once. Transfer steak to a cutting board and let sit for 5 minutes. Cut the butter mixture into slices and top the steak. Let the butter melt over before serving. Enjoy!

Paprika Breaded Beef

Serves: 1 | Total Time: 30 minutes

Ingredients

Celery salt to taste

1 (5 ounces) beef cube steak

1 tablespoon milk

¼ cup flour

¼ teaspoon paprika

1 small egg

¼ cup bread crumbs

1 teaspoon olive oil

Directions

Start by preheating your air fryer to 350°F. Place the cube steak in a zipper-sealed bag or between two sheets of cling wrap. Gently pound the steaks until they are slightly thinner. Set aside. In a bowl, mix together milk, flour, paprika, celery salt, and egg until just combined.

In a separate bowl, mix together the crumbs and olive oil. Take the steaks and dip them into the buttermilk batter, shake off the excess, and return to a plate for 5 minutes. Next, dip the steaks in the bread crumbs, patting the crumbs on both sides. Air Fry the steaks until the crust is crispy and brown, 12-16 minutes. Serve warm.

Air Fried Salisbury Steak Burger

Serves: 1 | Total Time: 35 minutes

Ingredients

1 tablespoon bread crumbs

1 teaspoon beef broth

¼ tablespoon cooking sherry

¼ tablespoon ketchup

¼ tablespoon Dijon mustard

¼ teaspoon Worcestershire sauce

¼ teaspoon onion powder

¼ teaspoon garlic powder

5 ounces ground beef

¼ cup sliced mushrooms

¼ tablespoon butter

1 bun, split and toasted

Directions

Preheat the air fryer to 375°F. Combine the bread crumbs, broth, cooking sherry, ketchup, mustard, Worcestershire sauce, garlic and onion powder and mix well. Add the beef and mix with your hands, then form into a burger and refrigerate while preparing the mushrooms.

Mix the mushrooms and butter in a pan. Place the pan in the air fryer and Bake for 8-10 minutes, stirring once, until the mushrooms are brown and tender. Remove and set aside.

Line the frying basket with round parchment paper and punch holes in it. Place the burger over the paper and cook it for 11-14 minutes or until cooked through. Put the burger on the bun bottom, top it with the mushrooms, then put the bun top. Enjoy!

Grilled Rib-Eye "a la Provence"

Serves: 1 | Total Time: 25 minutes

Ingredients

1 (4-oz) ribeye steak

¼ teaspoon herbs de Provence

Salt and black pepper to taste

Directions

Start by preheating your air fryer to 360°F. Season the steak with herbs, salt, and pepper. Place it in the greased frying basket and cook for 8-12 minutes, flipping once. Use a thermometer to check for doneness and adjust time as needed. Let the steak rest for a few minutes and serve.

Broccoli & Mushroom Strips

Serves: 1 | Total Time: 30 minutes

Ingredients

1 (5 ounces) sirloin strip steak, cubed

¼ cup sliced cremini mushrooms

½ tablespoon potato starch

2 teaspoons beef broth

¼ teaspoon soy sauce

1 cup broccoli florets

¼ onion, chopped

¼ tablespoon grated fresh ginger

¼ cup cooked quinoa

Directions

Add potato starch, broth, and soy sauce to a bowl and mix, then add in the beef and coat thoroughly. Marinate for 5 minutes.

Preheat your air fryer to 400°F. Remove the beef from the marinade and move it to the air fryer. Reserve the marinade. Add broccoli, onion, mushrooms, and ginger to the air fryer.

Bake all ingredients for 12-15 minutes until the beef is golden brown and the veggies are soft. Pour the reserved marinade over the beef. Cook for 2-3 more minutes until the sauce is bubbling. Serve over cooked quinoa.

Easy Beef & Spinach Sautée

Serves: 1 | Total Time: 30 minutes

Ingredients

½ tomato, chopped

1 teaspoon crumbled Goat cheese

5 ounces ground beef

¼ shallot, chopped

1 garlic clove, minced

½ cup baby spinach

1 teaspoon lemon juice

2 tablespoons beef broth

Directions

Start by preheating your air fryer to 370°F. Crumble the beef in a baking pan and place it in the air fryer. Air Fry for 3-7 minutes, stirring once. Drain the meat and make sure it's browned.

Toss in the tomato, shallot, and garlic and Air Fry for an additional 4-8 minutes until soft. Mix in the spinach, lemon juice, and beef broth and cook for 2-4 minutes until the spinach wilts. Top with goat cheese and serve.

Air Fried London Broil

Serves: 1 | Total Time: 25 minutes + marinating time

Ingredients

1 (5 ounces) top-round London broil steak

1 tablespoon soy sauce

¼ tablespoon balsamic vinegar

1 teaspoon olive oil

¼ tablespoon mustard

¼ teaspoon maple syrup

1 garlic clove, minced

¼ teaspoon dried oregano

Salt and black pepper to taste

¼ teaspoon smoked paprika

1 tablespoon red onions, chopped

Directions

Whisk soy sauce, mustard, vinegar, olive oil, maple oregano, syrup, oregano garlic, red onions, salt, pepper, and paprika in a small bowl. Put the steak in a shallow container and pour the marinade over the steak. Cover and let sit for 20 minutes.

Preheat your air fryer to 400°F. Transfer the steak to the frying basket and bake for 5 minutes. Flip the steak and bake for another 4-6 minutes. Allow sitting for 5 minutes before slicing. Enjoy.

Double Cheese & Beef Burger

Serves: 1 | Total Time: 30 minutes

Ingredients

1 toasted onion bun, split

1 teaspoon breadcrumbs

¼ tablespoon milk

¼ teaspoon smoked paprika

1 tablespoon salsa

¼ teaspoon cayenne pepper

¼ tablespoon grated Cotija cheese

5 ounces ground beef

1 Colby Jack cheese slice

1 tablespoon sour cream

Directions

Preheat the air fryer to 375°F. Combine the breadcrumbs, milk, paprika, cayenne, and Cotija cheese in a bowl and mix. Let stand for 5 minutes. Add the ground beef and mix with your hands. Form it into a patty and lay it on wax paper.

Place the patty into the greased frying basket and Air Fry for 11-14 minutes, flipping once during cooking until golden and crunchy on the outside. Put the slice of Colby jack on top and cook for another minute until the cheese melts.

Combine the salsa with sour cream. Spread the mix on the bun bottom, lay the patty on top, and spoon the rest of the mix over. Add the top bun and serve.

Mexican Lazy Pizza

Serves: 1 | Total Time: 35 minutes

Ingredients

¼ cup canned refried beans

½ cup shredded cheddar cheese

1 teaspoon chopped cilantro

2 teaspoons salsa

¼ red bell pepper, chopped

¼ sliced jalapeño

1 pizza crust

2 meatballs, halved

Directions

Preheat the air fryer to 375°F. Combine the refried beans, salsa, jalapeño, and bell pepper in a bowl and spread on the pizza crust. Top with meatball halves and sprinkle with cheddar cheese. Put the pizza in the greased frying basket and Bake for 7-10 minutes until hot and the cheese is brown. Sprinkle with fresh cilantro and serve.

Low-Carb Garlic & Butter Rib Eye Steak

Serves: 1 | Total Time: 25 minutes

Ingredients

1 (5 ounces) rib eye steak

Salt and black pepper to taste

¼ tablespoon butter

¼ teaspoon paprika

¼ tablespoon chopped rosemary

1 garlic clove, minced

¼ tablespoon chopped parsley

¼ tablespoon chopped mint

Directions

Start by preheating your air fryer to 400°F. Sprinkle salt and pepper on both sides of the rib eye. Transfer the rib eye to the greased frying basket, then top with butter, mint, paprika, rosemary, and garlic.

Bake for 6 minutes, then flip the steak. Bake for another 6 minutes. For medium-rare, the steak needs to reach an internal temperature of 140°F. Allow resting for 5 minutes before slicing. Serve sprinkled with parsley and enjoy!

Desert-Style Lamb Chops

Serves: 1 | Total Time: 25 minutes

Ingredients

3 lamb chops

1 cup breadcrumbs

1 egg, beaten

Salt and black pepper to taste

¼ tablespoon thyme

¼ tablespoon mint, chopped

¼ teaspoon garlic powder

¼ teaspoon ground rosemary

¼ teaspoon cayenne powder

¼ teaspoon ras el hanout

Directions

Start by preheating your air fryer to 320°F. Mix the breadcrumbs, thyme, mint, garlic, rosemary, cayenne, ras el hanout, salt, and pepper in a bowl. Dip the lamb chops in the beaten eggs, then coat with the crumb mixture. Air Fry for 14-16 minutes, turning once. Serve and enjoy!

Middle-Eastern Lamb Chops with Couscous

Serves: 1 | Total Time: 30 minutes

Ingredients

3 lamb chops

1 teaspoon olive oil

¼ teaspoon ground coriander

¼ teaspoon lemon zest

¼ teaspoon za'atar seasoning

1 garlic clove, minced

Salt and black pepper to taste

¼ cup couscous

Directions

Place the couscous in a bowl and cover with 3/4 cup of salted boiling water. Let sit until the water is absorbed.

Preheat your air fryer to 390°F. Coat the lamb chops with olive oil. Mix the mint leaves, coriander, lemon zest, za'atar, garlic, salt, and pepper in a bowl. Rub the seasoning onto the chops.

Place them in the greased frying basket and Air Fry for 14-16 minutes, flipping once. Let the lamb chops rest for a few minutes. Serve with the couscous.

OTHER FINGER FAVORITES

Classic Bacon-Wrapped Smokies

Serves: 1 | Total Time: 15 minutes

Ingredients

2 small smokies

2 bacon strips, sliced

Salt and black pepper to taste

Directions

Start by preheating your air fryer to 350°F. Wrap the bacon slices around the smokies. Arrange the rolls, seam side down, on the greased frying basket. Sprinkle with salt and pepper and Air Fry for 5-8 minutes, turning once until the bacon is crisp and juicy around them. Serve and enjoy!

Holiday Giant Nachos

Serves: 1 | Total Time: 20 minutes

Ingredients

2 tablespoons sour cream

½ teaspoon chili powder

Salt to taste

2 soft corn tortillas

2 teaspoons avocado oil

½ cup refried beans

¼ cup cheddar cheese shreds

2 tablespoons Parmesan cheese

2 tablespoons sliced black olives

¼ cup torn iceberg lettuce

¼ cup baby spinach

½ sliced avocado

1 tomato, diced

2 lime wedges

Directions

Start by preheating your air fryer to 400°F. Whisk the sour cream, chili powder, and salt in a small bowl. Brush tortillas with avocado oil and season one side with salt. Place tortillas in the frying basket and Bake for 3 minutes. Set aside.

Layer the refried beans, Parmesan and cheddar cheeses in the tortillas. Place them back into the basket and Bake for 2 minutes. Divide tortillas into 2 serving plates. Top each tortilla with black olives, baby spinach, lettuce, and tomatoes. Dollop sour cream mixture on each. Serve with lime and avocado wedges on the side.

Authentic Pigs in Blankets

Serves: 1 | Total Time: 30 minutes

Ingredients

¼ (8-oz) can crescent rolls

2 mini smoked hot dogs

½ tablespoon honey mustard

½ tablespoon mayonnaise

Directions

Start by preheating your air fryer to 380°F. Roll out the crescent roll dough and separate into 2 triangles. Cut each triangle in half. Place 1 hot dog at the base of the triangle and roll it up in the dough; gently press the tip in. Repeat for the rest of the rolls.

Place the rolls in the greased frying basket. Bake for 8-10 minutes. Mix the honey mustard and mayonnaise in a small bowl. Serve the hot dogs with the dip.

Hot & Breaded Cheese Sticks

Serves: 1 | Total Time: 20 minutes + freezing time

Ingredients

1 egg, beaten

2 teaspoons dried bread crumbs

½ tablespoon ground peanuts

¼ teaspoon chili powder

¼ teaspoon ground coriander

¼ teaspoon red pepper flakes

¼ teaspoon cayenne pepper

4 mozzarella cheese sticks

Directions

Preheat the air fryer to 375°F. Beat the egg in a bowl, and on a plate, combine the breadcrumbs, peanuts, coriander, chili powder, pepper flakes, and cayenne. Dip each piece of string cheese in the egg, then in the breadcrumb mix.

After lining a baking sheet with parchment paper, put the sticks on it and freeze them for 30 minutes. Get the sticks out of the freezer and set in the frying basket in a single layer.

Spritz them with cooking oil. Air Fry for 7-9 minutes until the exterior is golden and the interior is hot and melted. Serve hot with marinara or ranch sauce.

Air Fried Mozzarella Sticks

Serves: 1 | Total Time: 25 minutes

Ingredients

1 tablespoon flour

1 small egg

1 tablespoon milk

½ cup bread crumbs

¼ teaspoon salt

¼ teaspoon Italian seasoning

4 mozzarella sticks

2 teaspoons olive oil

2 tablespoons warm marinara sauce

Directions

Place the flour in a bowl. In another bowl, beat the egg and milk. In a third bowl, combine the crumbs, salt, and Italian seasoning. Cut the mozzarella sticks into thirds. Roll each piece in flour, then dredge in egg mixture, and finally roll in breadcrumb mixture. Shake off the excess between each step. Place them in the freezer for 10 minutes.

Preheat your air fryer to 400°F. Place mozzarella sticks in the frying basket and Air Fry for 5 minutes, shake twice and brush with olive oil. Serve the mozzarella sticks immediately with marinara sauce.

Italian-Style Fried Olives

Serves: 1 | Total Time: 25 minutes

Ingredients

4 pitted green olives

2 tablespoons all-purpose flour

Salt and black pepper to taste

½ teaspoon Italian seasoning

2 tablespoons bread crumbs

1 small egg

Directions

Start by preheating your air fryer to 400°F. Set out three small bowls. In the first, mix flour, Italian seasoning, salt, and pepper. In the bowl, beat the egg. In the third bowl, add bread crumbs.

Dip the olives in the flour, then the egg, then in the crumbs. When all of the olives are breaded, place them in the greased frying basket and Air Fry for 6 minutes. Turn them and cook for another 2 minutes or until brown and crispy. Serve chilled.

Eggplant & Parmesan Sticks

Serves: 1 | Total Time: 35 minutes

Ingredients

1 small egg

1 tablespoon heavy cream

2 tablespoons bread crumbs

½ teaspoon Italian seasoning

2 tablespoons grated Parmesan cheese

Salt to taste

1 eggplant, cut into sticks

½ cup tomato sauce, warm

Directions

Start by preheating your air fryer to 400°F. In a bowl, mix the eggs and heavy cream. In another bowl, combine bread crumbs, Parmesan cheese, Italian seasoning and salt. Dip eggplant fries in egg mixture and dredge them in crumb mixture.

Place the fries in the greased frying basket and Air Fry for 12 minutes, shaking once. Transfer to a large serving plate and serve with warmed tomato sauce.

Asian-Style Gingered Shoyu Tofu

Serves: 1 | Total Time: 25 minutes

Ingredients

¼ (8-oz) package extra-firm tofu, cubed

1 teaspoon shoyu

¼ teaspoon onion powder

¼ teaspoon garlic powder

¼ teaspoon ginger powder

¼ teaspoon turmeric powder

Black pepper to taste

½ tablespoon nutritional yeast

¼ teaspoon dried rosemary

¼ teaspoon dried dill

½ teaspoon cornstarch

1 teaspoon sunflower oil

Directions

Toss the tofu with shoyu. Add the onion, garlic, ginger, turmeric, and pepper. Gently toss to coat. Add the yeast, rosemary, dill, and cornstarch. Toss to coat. Dribble with the oil and toss again.

Preheat your air fryer to 390°F. Spray the fryer basket with oil, put the tofu in the basket and Bake for 7 minutes. Remove, shake gently, and cook for another 7 minutes or until the tofu is crispy.

Simple Thyme-Roasted Jicama

Serves: 1 | Total Time: 25 minutes

Ingredients

¼ pound jicama, cut into fries

1 tablespoon olive oil

Salt and black pepper to taste

1 garlic clove, minced

2 thyme sprigs

Directions

Start by preheating your air fryer to 360°F. Coat the jicamas with olive oil, salt, pepper, and garlic in a bowl. Pour the jicama fries into the frying basket and top with the thyme sprigs. Roast for 20 minutes, stirring twice. Remove the rosemary sprigs. Serve and enjoy!

Tangy Cherry Tomatoes

Serves: 1 | Total Time: 15 minutes

Ingredients

5 cherry tomatoes, halved

1 teaspoon olive oil

Sea salt to taste

1 teaspoon balsamic vinegar

Directions

Start by preheating your air fryer to 380°F. Combine all ingredients in a bowl. Arrange the cherry tomatoes on the frying basket and Bake for 8 minutes until the tomatoes are blistered, shaking once. Serve drizzled with balsamic vinegar.

Easy Green Beans

Serves: 1 | Total Time: 15 minutes

Ingredients

½ tablespoon tahini

½ tablespoon lemon juice

¼ teaspoon allspice

½ pound green beans, trimmed

Directions

Start by preheating your air fryer to 400°F. Whisk tahini, lemon juice, 1 tablespoon of water, and allspice in a bowl. Put in the green beans and toss to coat. Roast for 5 minutes until golden brown and cooked. Serve immediately.

Bacon-Wrapped Stuffed Dates

Serves: 1 | Total Time: 20 minutes

Ingredients

2 bacon slices, halved

4 pitted dates

½ tablespoon crumbled blue cheese

½ tablespoon cream cheese

Directions

Make a slit lengthways in each date. Mix the blue cheese and cream cheese in a small bowl. Add ½ teaspoon of cheese mixture to the center of each date. Wrap each date with a halved slice of bacon and seal with a toothpick.

Preheat your air fryer to 400°F. Place the dates on the bottom of the greased frying basket in a single layer. Bake for 6-8 minutes, flipping the dates once until the bacon is cooked and crispy. Allow to cool and serve warm.

Pancetta-Wrapped Asparagus

Serves: 1 | Total Time: 30 minutes

Ingredients

4 asparagus trimmed

Salt and pepper pepper

1 pancetta slice

1 tablespoon fresh sage, chopped

Directions

Sprinkle the asparagus with fresh sage, salt, and pepper. Toss to coat. Make a bundle of the spears by wrapping the center of the bunch with the pancetta slice.

Preheat your air fryer to 400°F. Put the bundle in the greased frying basket and Air Fry for 8-10 minutes or until the pancetta is brown and the asparagus are starting to char on the edges.

Broccoli Florets in Adobo

Serves: 1 | Total Time: 25 minutes

Ingredients

1 chipotle pepper in adobo sauce, minced

½ broccoli head, cut into florets

½ teaspoon chili oil

½ tablespoon adobo sauce

¼ teaspoon chili powder

Salt and black pepper to taste

Directions

Preheat the air fryer to 375°F. Combine the chili oil, chipotle pepper, adobo sauce, chili powder, salt, and pepper in a bowl and mix well. Add the broccoli and toss to coat evenly.

Put the broccoli in the frying basket and Air Fry for 13-18 minutes, shaking the basket once halfway through until the broccoli is crispy.

Authentic Sicilian Arancini

Serves: 1 | Total Time: 20 minutes

Ingredients

½ minced red bell pepper

1 teaspoon grated Parmesan cheese

½ cup cooked rice

1 small egg

1 tablespoon plain flour

½ finely grated carrot

1 tablespoon minced fresh parsley

1 teaspoon olive oil

Directions

Start by preheating your air fryer to 380°F. Add the rice, egg, and flour to a bowl and mix well. Add the carrots, bell peppers, parsley, and Parmesan cheese and mix again. Shape into 8 fritters.

Brush with olive oil and place the fritters in the frying basket. Air Fry for 8-10 minutes, turning once, until golden. Serve hot and enjoy!

Continental Radish Wedges

Serves: 1 | Total Time: 20 minutes

Ingredients

1 tablespoon butter, melted

1 garlic clove, minced

Salt to taste

5 radishes, quartered

1 tablespoon feta cheese crumbles

1 tablespoon chopped parsley

Directions

Start by preheating your air fryer to 370°F. Mix the butter, garlic, and salt in a bowl. Stir in radishes. Place the radish wedges in the frying basket and Roast for 10 minutes, shaking once. Transfer to a large serving dish and stir in feta cheese. Scatter with parsley and serve.

Air Fried Fennel Slices

Serves: 1 | Total Time: 15 minutes

Ingredients

½ fennel bulb

1 teaspoon olive oil

Salt to taste

1 lemon wedge

½ teaspoon fennel seeds

Directions

Start by preheating your air fryer to 350°F. Remove the fronds from the fennel bulb and reserve them. Cut the fennel into thin slices. Rub fennel chips with olive oil on both sides and sprinkle with salt and fennel seeds. Place fennel slices in the frying basket and Bake for 8 minutes. Squeeze lemon on top and scatter with chopped fronds. Serve.

French-Style Brussels Sprouts with Saffron Aioli

Serves: 1 | Total Time: 20 minutes

Ingredients

½ pound Brussels sprouts, halved

¼ teaspoon garlic powder

Salt and black pepper to taste

¼ cup mayonnaise

½ tablespoon olive oil

½ tablespoon Dijon mustard

½ teaspoon minced garlic

Salt and black pepper to taste

¼ teaspoon liquid saffron

Directions

Start by preheating your air fryer to 380°F. Combine the Brussels sprouts, garlic powder, salt, and pepper in a large bowl. Place in the fryer and spray with cooking oil. Bake for 12-14 minutes, shaking once, until just brown.

Meanwhile, in a small bowl, mix mayonnaise, olive oil, mustard, garlic, saffron, salt, and pepper. When the Brussels sprouts are slightly cool, serve with aioli. Enjoy!

Parmesan & Pumpkin Cubes

Serves: 1 | Total Time: 35 minutes

Ingredients

1 cup pumpkin cubes

1 tablespoon olive oil

Salt and black pepper to taste

¼ teaspoon pumpkin pie spice

¼ tablespoon thyme

½ tablespoon grated Parmesan cheese

Directions

Start by preheating your air fryer to 360°F. Put the cubed pumpkin with olive oil, salt, pumpkin pie spice, black pepper, and thyme in a bowl and stir until the pumpkin is well coated.

Pour this mixture into the frying basket and Roast for 18-20 minutes, stirring once. Sprinkle the pumpkin with grated Parmesan. Serve and enjoy!

Cinnamon Sweet Potato Fries

Serves: 1 | Total Time: 30 minutes

Ingredients

1 sweet potato

1 teaspoon butter, melted

¼ teaspoon cinnamon

Salt and black pepper to taste

Directions

Start by preheating your air fryer to 400°F. Peel the potato and slice it thinly crosswise. Transfer the slices to a large bowl. Toss with butter, cinnamon, salt, and pepper until fully coated.

Place half of the slices into the air fryer. Stacking is ok. Air Fry for 10 minutes. Shake the basket, and cook for another 10 -12 minutes until crispy. Serve hot.

Swiss-Style Potato

Serves: 1 | Total Time: 55 minutes

Ingredients

1 whole potato

1 teaspoon olive oil

Salt to taste

½ tablespoon minced garlic

1 teaspoon parsley, chopped

2 oz grated Swiss cheese

Directions

Start by preheating your air fryer to 390°F. Prick the potato all over using a fork. Drizzle with olive oil all over the skins and rub it with minced garlic, salt, and parsley.

Place the potato in the frying basket and Bake for 20-25 minutes or until tender. Remove the potato from the basket and serve it along with grated Swiss cheese. Serve.

Chipotle Avocado Wedges

Serves: 1 | Total Time: 15 minutes

Ingredients

¼ teaspoon smoked paprika

1 teaspoon olive oil

¼ lime, juiced

4 peeled avocado wedges

¼ teaspoon chipotle powder

Salt to taste

Directions

Start by preheating your air fryer to 400°F. Drizzle the avocado wedges with olive oil and lime juice. In a bowl, combine chipotle powder, smoked paprika, and salt. Sprinkle over the avocado wedges. Place them in the frying basket and Air Fry for 7 minutes. Serve immediately.

Sweet Brussels Sprouts

Serves: 1 | Total Time: 15 minutes

Ingredients

½ lb Brussels sprouts, quartered

1 teaspoon balsamic vinegar

1 teaspoon olive oil

1 teaspoon honey

Salt and black pepper to taste

½ tablespoon lime juice

Parsley for sprinkling

Directions

Start by preheating your air fryer to 350°F. Combine all ingredients in a bowl. Transfer them to the frying basket. Air Fry for 10 minutes, tossing once. Top with lime juice and parsley.

Spicy Okra Wedges

Serves: 1 | Total Time: 35 minutes

Ingredients

1 cup okra, sliced

½ cup breadcrumbs

1 egg, beaten

A pinch of black pepper

¼ teaspoon crushed red peppers

1 teaspoon hot Tabasco sauce

Directions

Start by preheating your air fryer to 350°F. Place the eggs and Tabasco sauce in a bowl and stir; set aside. In a separate mixing bowl, combine the breadcrumbs, crushed peppers, and pepper.

Dip the okra into the beaten eggs, then coat in the crumb mixture. Lay the okra pieces on the greased frying basket. Air Fry for 14-16 minutes, shaking the basket several times during cooking. When ready, the okra will be crispy and golden brown. Serve.

Balsamic-Roasted Asparagus

Serves: 1 | Total Time: 20 minutes

Ingredients

6 asparagus, trimmed

1 teaspoon olive oil

1 garlic clove, minced

1 tablespoon balsamic vinegar

¼ teaspoon dried thyme

¼ red chili, finely sliced

Directions

Start by preheating your air fryer to 380°F. Put the asparagus and olive oil in a bowl and stir to coat, then put them in the frying basket. Toss some garlic over the asparagus.

Roast for 4-8 minutes until crisp-tender. Spritz with balsamic vinegar and toss in some thyme leaves. Top with red chili slices and serve.

Eggplant Rounds the Italian Way

Serves: 1 | Total Time: 30 minutes

Ingredients

1 eggplant, sliced into rounds

1 egg

½ cup bread crumbs

1 teaspoon onion powder

¼ teaspoon Italian seasoning

¼ teaspoon garlic salt

¼ teaspoon paprika

1 tablespoon olive oil

Directions

Start by preheating your air fryer to 360°F. Whisk the egg and 1 tablespoon of water in a bowl until frothy. Mix the bread crumbs, onion powder, Italian seasoning, salt, and paprika separately.

Dip the eggplant slices into the egg mixture, then coat them with the bread crumb mixture. Put the slices in a single layer in the frying basket. Drizzle with olive oil. Air Fry for 23-25 minutes, turning once. Serve and enjoy!

Buffalo Russet Fries

Serves: 1 | Total Time: 35 minutes

Ingredients

1 russet potato
½ tablespoon buffalo sauce

1 teaspoon extra-virgin olive oil
Salt and black pepper to taste

Directions

Start by preheating your air fryer to 380°F. Peel and cut potato lengthwise into French fries. Place them in a bowl, then coat with olive oil, salt, and pepper. Air Fry them for 10 minutes. Shake the basket, then cook for five minutes. Serve drizzled with Buffalo sauce immediately.

Balsamic Beet Chips

Serves: 1 | Total Time: 40 minutes

Ingredients

¼ teaspoon balsamic vinegar
1 beet, peeled and sliced
1 garlic clove, minced

1 teaspoon chopped mint
Salt and black pepper to taste
1 tablespoon olive oil

Directions

Start by preheating your air fryer to 380°F. Coat all ingredients in a bowl, except balsamic vinegar. Pour the beet mixture into the frying basket and Roast for 25-30 minutes, stirring once. Serve, drizzled with vinegar and enjoy!

Potato Skins in Alfredo Sauce

Serves: 1 | Total Time: 50 minutes

Ingredients

1 russet potato, halved lengthwise
1 teaspoon grated Parmesan cheese

2 tablespoons Alfredo sauce
2 scallions, chopped

Directions

Start by preheating your air fryer to 400°F. Wrap each potato, cut-side down with parchment paper, and Roast for 30 minutes.

Carefully scoop out the potato flesh, leaving ¼-inch meat, and place it in a bowl. Stir in Alfredo sauce, scallions, and Parmesan cheese until well combined. Fill each potato skin with the cheese mixture and Grill for 3-4 minutes until crispy. Serve right away.

Five-Spice Potato Fries

Serves: 1 | Total Time: 30 minutes

Ingredients

1 Yukon Gold potato, cut into fries
¼ teaspoon Chinese five-spice
1 teaspoon coconut oil
½ teaspoon coconut sugar

¼ teaspoon garlic powder
Salt to taste
¼ teaspoon turmeric
¼ teaspoon paprika

Directions

Start by preheating your air fryer to 390°F. Place the coconut oil, sugar, garlic, Chinese five-spice, salt, turmeric, and paprika in a bowl and add the potato; toss to coat. Transfer the to the greased frying basket and Air Fry for 20-25 minutes, tossing twice until softened and golden. Serve warm.

Curry & Sour Cream Sweet Potato

Serves: 1 | Total Time: 20 minutes

Ingredients

¼ cup sour cream
¼ cup peach chutney
¼ teaspoon curry powder

1 sweet potato, julienned
1 tablespoon olive oil
Salt and black pepper to taste

Directions

Start by preheating your air fryer to 390°F. Mix together sour cream, peach chutney, and curry powder in a small bowl. Set aside. In a medium bowl, add sweet potato, olive oil, salt, and pepper. Toss to coat. Place the potatoes in the frying basket.

Bake for about 6 minutes, then shake the basket once. Cook for an additional 4 -6 minutes or until the potatoes are golden and crispy. Serve the fries hot in a basket along with the chutney sauce.

Hungarian-Style Super Spicy Fries

Serves: 1 | Total Time: 30 minutes

Ingredients

2 russet potatoes, peeled
1 tablespoon olive oil
¼ teaspoon chili powder

¼ teaspoon garlic powder
¼ teaspoon Hungarian paprika
Salt and black pepper to taste

Directions

Preheat the air fryer to 400°F. Using the spiralizer, cut the potatoes into 5-inch lengths and add them to a large bowl. Pour cold water, cover, and set aside for 30 minutes. Drain and dry with a kitchen towel, then toss back in the bowl.

Drizzle the potatoes with olive oil and season with salt, pepper, chili, garlic, and paprika. Toss well. Put the potatoes in the frying basket and Air Fry for 10-12 minutes, shaking the basket once until the potatoes are golden and crispy. Serve warm and enjoy!

Extra Crunchy Sweet Potato Fries

Serves: 1 | Total Time: 35 minutes

Ingredients

1 sweet potato, peeled
½ tablespoon cornstarch
½ teaspoon canola oil
½ teaspoon olive oil

¼ teaspoon smoked paprika
¼ teaspoon garlic powder
Salt and black pepper to taste
¼ cup cocktail sauce

Directions

Cut the potato lengthwise to form French fries. Put in a resealable plastic bag and add cornstarch. Seal and shake to coat the fries. Combine the canola oil, olive oil, paprika, garlic powder, salt, and pepper fries in a large bowl. Add the sweet potato fries and mix to combine.

Start by preheating your air fryer to 380°F. Place fries in the greased basket and fry for 20-25 minutes, shaking the basket once until crisp. Drizzle with Cocktail sauce to serve.

AIR FRYER COOKING TIMES (APPROXIMATE)

POULTRY	TEMPERATURE	COOKING TIME
Chicken Wings	400°F / 200°C	15-20 minutes
Boneless Chicken Breasts	380°F / 190°C	15-20 minutes
Chicken Drumsticks	400°F / 200°C	20-25 min
Boneless Chicken Thighs	400°F / 200°C	15-20 minutes
Chicken Tenders	400°F / 200°C	8-10 minutes
Whole Chicken	360°F / 180°C	55-65 minutes
Frozen Chicken Nuggets	400°F / 200°C	10-13 minutes
Cornish Game Hen	360°F / 180°C	30-35 minutes
Boneless Turkey Breasts	360°F / 180°C	45-55 minutes
Turkey Meatballs	400°F / 200°C	8-12 minutes
BEEF	**TEMPERATURE**	**COOKING TIME**
Ribeye Steak	400°F / 200°C	12-15 minutes
Sirloin Steak	400°F / 200°C	12-15 minutes
Round Top Roast	400°F / 200°C	40-55 minutes
Steak Bites	400°F / 200°C	10-13 minutes
Meatballs	400°F / 200°C	10-13 minutes
Burgers	350°F / 180°C	12-15 minutes
Filet Mignon	400°F / 200°C	15-20 minutes
PORK	**TEMPERATURE**	**COOKING TIME**
Ribs	400°F / 200°C	25-35 minutes
Pork Chops	400°F / 200°C	13-15 minutes
Pork Tenderloin	400°F / 200°C	13-15 minutes
Pork Loin	400°F / 200°C	50-55 minutes
Sausages	400°F / 200°C	13-15 minutes
Bacon	400°F / 200°C	8-12 minutes
SEAFOOD	**TEMPERATURE**	**COOKING TIME**
Salmon	400°F / 200°C	10-15 minutes
Fish Fillet	400°F / 200°C	8-12 minutes
Tuna Steak	400°F / 200°C	8-12 minutes
Shrimp	380°F / 190°C	8-12 minutes
Scallops	380°F / 190°C	6-9 minutes
Crab Legs	380°F / 190°C	5-8 minutes
Lobster Tail	400°F / 200°C	6-9 minutes
Frozen Fish Sticks	400°F / 200°C	10-13 minutes

VEGETABLES	TEMPERATURE	COOKING TIME
Brussels Sprouts	400°F / 200°C	8-12 minutes
Carrots	400°F / 200°C	10-12 minutes
Asparagus	400°F / 200°C	6-8 minutes
Green Beans	400°F / 200°C	6-8 minutes
Broccoli	400°F / 200°C	6-8 minutes
Cauliflower	400°F / 200°C	6-8 minutes
Whole Potatoes	400°F / 200°C	45-55 minutes
Potato Wedges	400°F / 200°C	20-25 minutes
Frozen Fries	400°F / 200°C	15-18 minutes
Corn on the cob	400°F / 200°C	10-13 minutes
Zucchini	400°F / 200°C	6-8 minutes
Eggplant	400°F / 200°C	6-8 minutes

ADD YOUR FOOD ITEM	TEMPERATURE	COOKING TIME

NOTES

Made in the USA
Monee, IL
07 November 2024